WISH ME WELL

Notes on My Sleeve

WISH ME WELL

Notes on My Sleeve

MICK HANLY

Gill & Macmillan

Gill & Macmillan Ltd
Hume Avenue, Park West, Dublin 12
with associated companies throughout the world
www.gillmacmillan.ie
© Mick Hanly 2005
0 7171 3890 9
Design by DesignLab, Dublin
Print origination by Carole Lynch
Printed by GraphyCems, Spain

This book is typeset in Venetian 301BT 13pt on 16pt.

The paper used in this book comes from the wood pulp of managed forests.
For every tree felled, at least one tree is planted,
thereby renewing natural resources.

A CIP catalogue record for this book is available
from the British Library.

1 3 5 4 2

Song lyrics printed by permission of
Doghouse Songs Limited

To Marie

CONTENTS

Songs

ACKNOWLEDGMENTS

I would like to thank the people who helped me with this book. Poet Michael Coady, whose poem 'The Letter' from his book *All Souls* was my inspiration, and whose encouragement and help in editing was invaluable; my brother David, who was also constant in his encouragement — he pruned mercilessly, but always ended with the words 'onward and upward'; my fellow musician Declan Sinnott, without whose generosity and skill there wouldn't be an album, and no reason to write these 'Notes On My Sleeve'; my wife Marie, whose love and patience knows no limits.

There were also many others who had honest and encouraging words to offer. Thank you all. Finally, my thanks to Fergal Tobin and the staff at Gill & Macmillan.

Onward and upward!

INTRODUCTION

I haven't written a song in six months. It's been a barren time, but it hasn't been entirely wasted. I've been busy, engaged in something akin to a game of Trivial Pursuit®. I've been researching the songs on my forthcoming album, *Wish Me Well*. Nothing odd in that: how do you write a bunch of songs that you deem to be thoughtful and enquiring, without giving them some thought? Thing is, I've started the research after the songs have been written, but that's not wholly accurate; I should say that, I've gone back to the ragbag confusion that gave rise to the songs in the first place and tried to put the journey towards completion on paper. It's been an interesting journey. Many times, along the way, I've doubted myself, and believed that the whole experiment was indeed a trivial pursuit. If the phrase 'I've started, so I'll finish' had not been ringing in my ears throughout, I might have walked away and tidied the garden, but someone had to write the sleeve notes, and I've assigned that task to myself, one more time.

So, I've been getting up at five o'clock every morning to do this for a couple of hours, and despite the self-doubt, and the emotional unearthing of quite a number of skeletons, I've enjoyed the experience. And why such copious and comprehensive sleeve notes? Well, I can think of three reasons straight off that make sense to me, though they may not make much sense to you.

Firstly, *Wish Me Well* was started in 2001, and as I write, it's still not in the can. The reason for this is that the producer of the album, Declan Sinnott, guitarist supreme, musician extraordinaire, and all-round wonderful man, is a perfectionist, and

I'm a musical *mullocker*. That part of me which aspires to perfection is very pleased that we've chosen this route: the mullocker finds it hugely frustrating, but the creative part of me has found the whole exercise rewarding. What began as a project to revisit the best of my old songs and place them in new settings has become an album with eight new songs, and a fresh stab at three older ones. There are no basement tapes, but the bin has been emptied daily. Most of the stuff I write doesn't make it to the basement; it's binned before it gets the chance to waste other people's time.

The album won't be finished until Declan is happy, and he's not going to be happy until he feels that I'm happy. On day one, this was the deal we shook hands on, and if the album is not finished until 2020, then so be it, and if as a consequence, the last six months of scribbling and introspection have to be put on some very hard ice, then, so be that too.

Secondly, I played a gig in The Brewery Lane Theatre in Carrick-on-Suir in March 2003, where I met the poet, Michael Coady. I hope the next gig will be as enjoyable as the last, and that I'll get to meet Michael again, because I need to tell him that I've used the blueprint for one of his poems for this project. In 1997 Michael published a book of poems and stories called *All Souls*, in which is to be found the poem, 'The Letter'. This poem, and its accompanying history, is one of the most moving pieces of work that I've ever read. Read it, and your life will be enriched.

When I finished writing 'Shellakabookee Boy', which is a song about my stepson Thomas, I immediately thought of 'The Letter'. In a vague way I thought that I could outline the plot and the origins of 'Shellakabookee Boy' in the same way that Michael did with 'The Letter'.

The real songwriter's sales pitch opportunity is extremely brief. At most, a three to four minute interval in which to plant that emotional, treble-twenty dart which makes the listener listen. He might not have the benefit of a good interpreter, or fancy décolletage with which to arrest, but if his song is to pass muster, the word-and-music marriage must hit the spot before the static of the world re-engages the ear. So all addendums and explanations are superfluous. A song must have its own feet, or else it keels over.

Most of my efforts have tended to steal an extra minute, sometimes two, and radio tends to shy away from anything over the four-minute mark. There are exceptions: 'Hey Jude' (7 minutes 42 seconds) and 'McArthur Park' (7 minutes 24 seconds) both break the four-minute rule, but are so loaded with emotional arrows that they bypass the radio 'embargo' with ease. Whether the five-minutes-plus songs on *Wish Me Well* will make it past the 'embargo' is a question I don't ask myself, but I live in hope.

Thirdly, I had an accident. Guitar players should not mow the lawn. I'm not going to give you the gory details, suffice it to say that the wonderful Accident and Emergency staff of St Luke's Hospital in Kilkenny had to put five stitches in the second finger of my left hand; yes, that's the one that has spent the last 30 years pressing down on the third, fourth and fifth strings of my Hagstrom guitar, and latterly, my Taylor. Suddenly I couldn't write songs because I couldn't prop up whatever tune I stumbled on. So, it was this; written in biro, with the good hand, while the other whined and whimpered.

I'm not being falsely modest when I say that I have to pinch myself mentally every time someone refers to me as a songwriter. I'm not sure that I deserve it, and further, I'm not sure that it's accurate. I think storyteller might be more appropriate. You see, when I think of songwriters, the names that spring to mind are Gershwin, Harte, Sondheim, Harburg, Lennon and McCartney, Dylan, Bart, Newman, Mitchell; the list is endless, but these are the greats, with classics and standards appearing to fall from their pens like confetti.

Their choruses and hooks have become as familiar as the streets we were born in, reference points on the roadmaps of our lives; reassuring, balming words that spring to mind on solitary train journeys, or burst into life by fireside or seaside. These songs are familiar touchstones that we return to time and time again because they wear the years so well. They continue to speak to us with a freshness, a relevance and a vitality that's unquenchable. They get slaughtered, murdered, crucified, flogged and *karaokied* to within an inch of their lives by tuneless truckers, finger-frozen brickies, vacuuming housewives, moneybag-toting curates; and that's in sobriety. In drunkenness, they suffer death by a thousand cuts and still manage to rise again like newly-sprung roses, ready for more punishment.

I don't write songs like that, hence my uncertainty about the songwriter label. I've written hundreds of tales in song form, one of which, to my astonishment, became the mainstay of a sizeable number of American juke-boxes during the 90s, and a staple of the cabaret diet here in Ireland. Yet you'd be hard put to find someone who could sing the chorus without faltering. But 'Things', now there's a different story. If you were to offer a cent to everyone who could sing:

'*Things, like a walk in the park.*
Things, like a kiss in the dark.
Things, like a sailboat ride.
What about the night we cried?'

you'd be a poor man. And 'Things' is no standard.

In spite of my doubts about my song-writing, I like to think that the songs on *Wish Me Well* have their own legs, and that this exercise is purely extra information; longer than usual sleeve notes. What started with Michael Coady's blueprint has staggered and strayed. In some of the stories I've changed the names of certain characters, in deference to the living and the dead, but at all times I've tried to give an honest picture of where this storyteller is coming from. I'm a glutton for sleeve notes myself, and I'm hoping that these will satisfy even the most voracious sleeve-note reader.

I Feel I Should Be Calling You

In 1983, photographer Fergus Bourke took a photograph of myself and my brother David for 'Kindred', a series in which one relation penned a portrait of the other for *The Sunday Tribune*. David wrote a very flattering piece about me, which he closed with a question of my father's:

'If he's as good as they say he is, why is he so poor?'

Unfortunately, on the day that the photograph was taken, I was wearing a wool jacket which had a hole in the sleeve, and when the picture appeared some weeks later, my mother's first question to me was:

'Had you nothing else to wear?'

I did have other jackets, without holes, but my daily wardrobe is dictated by temperature and comfort, and the wool jacket with the hole won the day.

To my parents, the photograph was just further proof of the imprudence of my decision to try and earn my living from the thing I loved, music.

'You had a grand job in the ESB,' my mother would chime every three years or so, my precarious financial situation not having improved since the last chiming.

'I wasn't happy in the ESB, Mam, end of story,' I'd say, defensively.

I didn't like being reminded that, for the majority, the music business is insecure, badly paid and, sometimes, future-less.

'I suppose,' she'd sigh. My pursuit of something as vague as a music career puzzled my parents. A song-writing career puzzled them even more. Surely after fifteen years of chasing around the country at all hours of the night and day, I should at least have a decent car, a home, and be surrounded by some of the material trappings of success, instead of cycling back and forth to the dole office, in a wool jacket with a hole in it, living in a rented house in Fairview, my first marriage in shreds and my daughter Jessie in my care. They were confused.

'I saw your boy on the telly, Mary, he's doing great for himself, God bless him.'

'I heard your Michael on with Gay Byrnes (Gay Byrne) the other morning, I suppose he's in Dublin all the time now, Mary, is he?'

To the neighbours in St Patrick's Road, Limerick, 'being in Dublin all the time' and being interviewed by Gay Byrne was success. My parents, however, knew different. My profile belied my reality. When I did buy a car, it was an old Rover that spent more time in garages around the country than out-side my house. I kept hoping that my ship would come in. I also believed that one day it would, but whether my parents would be at the quayside to welcome it with me was a question I couldn't answer. As it turned out they missed its arrival by six months.

In September 1989, David called me to say that our father was in intensive care in Barrington's Hospital. He'd gone in for a routine check-up and had suffered major coronary failure in the bed. The patient in the bed next to him noticed the flashing light and pressed his own emergency bell. They came with all haste and pounded my 78-year-old father back to life. When he was breathing again, they moved him to intensive care and made the appropriate phone calls informing his kin that he was very unwell: the prognosis wasn't great. I don't know any of the nurses or interns that were involved in the pounding of my father back to life, but I'm certain that they are conscientious and generous to a fault, and I'd love to have them in my corner right now were my own heart to hiccup. But I have a problem with the resurrection of a 78-year-old, even if it is my own father. I can't quote the Hippocratic oath, but I think I understand the gist, and I find it all very noble, but there are times when I find a blinkered adherence to it is wrong.

My father had a good innings. For a year or two before he went into Barrington's for that check-up he was having 'little turns'. Unknown to us, these were a series of minor strokes, each one scarring and weakening his heart irreparably. Prior to this he was a healthy and lively man. He went on a six-mile walk every Sunday with a bunch of his men friends, whom he christened Dad's Army. He ran the errands for my mother and walked his dog twice a day. He could still mentally tot a grocery bill with speed, and got angry when rugby players Fergus Slattery or Brendan Mullen didn't part with the ball. He was alive. Then, as a result of the 'little turns', he was obliged to take drugs for his blood pressure. Then he had to take another drug to counteract the effect that the blood pressure drug was having on his balance, and suddenly he was flattened.

'They have me murdered,' he'd say resignedly, from his armchair.

David and I now took turns to drive to Limerick, and do the shopping and cooking on the weekends when the need arose. This was to relieve my sisters Dolores and Anne who were more or less on call and carried most of the burden. My other brothers, Noel and Seán, were out of the country. On one such weekend I asked my father what he thought of Ireland's chances against France.

'When is that on, Mike?' he asked.

It gave me a jolt. I suddenly realised that the lover of the 'crooked ball' was losing touch. We watched the game together, but despite a few poor refereeing decisions, he didn't bay angrily at the box and the game wasn't long into the second half when he nodded off. Dolores reported that when his dog died, it didn't upset him unduly, so David's call did not come as a surprise.

David came over to my rented house in Gracepark Terrace that afternoon with a bottle of gin. We drank it and recalled the man. By the time I'd thrown the empty bottle in the bin, we had decided, once again, that my father was a unique man, and an honourable one. We also made the mistake of burying him before he was dead. Let me try to describe the odd lover of the 'crooked ball'.

John Hanly was a man of average height (5'11") and average weight (13½ stone). He was always neat and well turned out in public. He was conscious of his weight, and didn't like having the small surplus that he carried on his tummy. He scolded my mother every time she put an extra potato on his plate. When the scolding was done he proceeded to eat it. He was going bald in his wedding photograph at the age of 27. He was wholly bald on top at 30, but he continued to tend some silver wisps that crossed his crown. He always wore something on his head; a cap to work, a hat to Mass, a knotted handkerchief to the beach, if he'd forgotten his headwear, and countless dabs of Mercurochrome, which he called 'the red stuff'. These dabs covered the results of bangs and scrapes that he'd received as a result of unplanned encounters with doors of presses and utensils that he'd hung from the roof of the shed. He hit everything that dangled six feet above the ground.

He drank and smoked, and here's where the oddness begins. He drove his Morris Minor to the pub each evening to have two pints and a small one. Then he drove home to smoke three of my mother's Gold Flake. He inhaled deeply and smoked a Gold Flake in half the time that it took me to smoke a John Player. By the time the stub of the third Gold Flake was carefully put in the fire, he was stoned. He was incapable of saying anything other than 'that's alright, lovee' or 'ok, lovee'. He usually said his night prayers in the kitchen. He knelt on one of the kitchen chairs and faced the wall for ten minutes. In later years he gave up going to the pub and took his tipple at home. He also upped his cigarette intake from three to four. When he'd reach for the fourth Gold Flake my mother would say,

'Is that another cigarette you're smoking, Johnny?'

''Tis, lovee.'

He checked and rechecked the locks on the windows. When my mother put the milk jug on the table for her cuppa before bed, he put it back in the fridge when her back was turned.

'Johnny, did you put away the milk on me?'

'Sorry, lovee.'

As soon as my father put a drop of alcohol to his lips, he changed utterly. He relaxed for the first time in the day, as the tension that possessed him dissipated. As a child I was quick to notice this transformation and usually chose the moment to make a request.

'Dad, can I keep pigeons? I have a house for 'em, an' everything.'

'I suppose so, lovee.'

Unfortunately, this beautiful mood was slept off and by morning he was back to normal. As the pigeons flapped from shed to roof, he wondered what had possessed him to allow such filthy creatures about the place.

My father was scrupulously honest. He spent all his life working in Matterson's Bacon Factory in Limerick, and rose from office boy to become their sales rep for the city. Having worked in all departments, he knew what could be promised and what could be delivered. His customers valued this, and responded with large orders, which left the other Matterson reps trailing in his wake. He was also generous. He was generous to us as children with his time and whatever spare money he had. If the weather was fine, he took us to the Garrison Wall, on Plassey River, to swim. He did this after a full day's work, and one particularly good summer he did it almost every evening for six weeks. He was forever putting his hand in his pocket for the price of a comic, the pictures or a new hurley.

'Ye must think I'm made of money,' he'd say.

He was also quick-tempered. He never laid a hand on my mother, but he clattered all of us from time to time. Our transgressions were small and the punishment often excessive. If you spilled a cup of tea at the table, you might ship a blow that would knock you out of your chair. If you were unable to control your giggles, in the back of the Morris Minor, you tried his patience. If you knocked over his pot of paint, you had to run for the hills. I hated the unpredictability of his temper, and for a long time I was frightened of him. He mellowed with age, and my brother Seán, who is twelve years younger than me, has a very different memory of him.

While I was still in primary school, my mother cycled to town every Saturday morning for the 'messages'. In her absence I washed the breakfast dishes, set the fire and swept the floor. When she got home, she'd put the full message bags on the kitchen table, survey the clean-up, and say,

'God, all the jobs done. Michael, I don't know what I'd do only for you.'

These were the words I craved. I loved her praise more than cowboys and indians, football, bows and arrows.

'Put on the kettle there for me, and off you go. My tongue is hanging out for a cup of tea.'

She loved tea. It accompanied her every pause in her full day. When she went on the Augustinian pilgrimage to Knock, she complained about the bad quality of the tea on the train. If she visited friends or neighbours and the tea didn't pass muster, she called it 'excursion tea'. She drank it in bed before she got up, and last thing before she went to bed at night.

She abhorred alcohol. She was frightened by what the abuse of it could do. When she was 35 she started smoking. Her weekly treat was a visit to the Savoy Cinema on Sunday nights, no matter what movie was showing. She went with a bevy of girlfriends and wore what she called her 'finery'. They taught her to smoke. She didn't inhale, so the habit didn't do her much harm, but she had pangs of conscience about the money she spent on it. I loved to see her in her finery. I loved her perfume and her beauty. I'd like to have been able to tell her how lovely she looked, but I didn't have the vocabulary. She was the engine-house of our home. She cooked and laundered for all of us with devotion and good humour. She mended, dusted, shopped, baked, gardened — between Masses, Novenas, excursions and picnics. She visited sick cousins and well cousins. In the early days of her marriage she had no kitchen appliances, save the kettle and the Jackson cooker. She had a washboard, a garden clothes-line and a wooden horse for the laundry. Everything was done by hand. She laughed heartily and I loved to hear her laughing.

When I was twelve our relationship suffered a serious set-back. I was caught stealing two bags of Tayto Crisps from a shop in Janesboro called Connery's. The stealing had been going on for some time, and a neighbour's child and I were the ones to be caught. The Guards called to the neighbour's house, and his father came to our door to inform my parents of my crime. The misdeed was complicated by the fact that Mrs Connery was one of my father's customers. We were driven to Janesboro, to apologise and make reparation.

When I got home my mother ran me to the bathroom and attacked me with the dowel of a wooden towel rack. She beat me until she exhausted herself. I screamed and begged her to stop, but she was unable. She was momentarily possessed by some demon and the rest of the family were so shocked that they felt unable to intervene.

This loss of control was completely out of character for my mother. I suspect that there was some other pressure that we knew nothing about troubling her at the time; my bringing the Guards to the door pushed her past breaking point. After the beating I didn't know where I stood anymore. I was uncertain of her love and she didn't have the language to reassure me that it was safe again. I slunk around the house wondering why I was so bad as to deserve such a beating. This very large skeleton was closeted and never mentioned.

I was into my 30s before I brought the memory up at

the dinner table one day. There was just my mother, father and I.

'Mam, do you remember when you gave me the hiding for stealing from Connery's shop?'

'God, I have no memory of that.'

'You must,' I insisted.

'No, Michael, I can't remember that, love.'

I would have been happy to accept that and be glad that she wasn't as haunted by the incident as I, but for the fact that my father said, in her absence,

'She never stops talking about that.'

'What do you mean?'

'She's always going on about that in bed. "How did I do that to my Michael?" she says.'

I find this heartbreaking. I tried again to bring the matter into the open about a year before she died, assuring her that I bore her no ill-will, and that I loved her dearly, but she insisted that she couldn't recall.

When she was 44, she caught a rare virus which damaged her heart and left her frightened for the rest of her life. I remember my father's anxiety when the doctors were unable to diagnose the illness, or give him a prognosis. When she emerged from the Richmond Hospital, in Dublin, she couldn't remember nouns and her bedtime reading was a struggle. She was put on a stabilising drug called Stelazine, which took away her facility to shed tears. Her hearty laugh also disappeared, and she was never the same again.

'You owe me for bread, two pounds of sugar, and ten Gold Flake.'

'I thought that I gave you the money for the Gold Flake before I went out to the Novena on Thursday?'

'You gave me no money on Thursday.'

'I could have sworn that I gave you the money for the cigarettes.'

'Sure how could you have given me the money for the cigarettes? I had five pounds seven and six in my pocket. I gave Fonsie Bennis three shillings for the Pools, I paid for the Mass card for Maggie Byrnes, and I gave you back the money that you paid to Paddy Reidy for the coal. Look, I have two pounds eleven and six in my pocket. I'll count it out for you.'

'There's no need for you to do that, Johnny. I could have sworn I gave you that; isn't that a mystery?'

'Check your purse again, let you.'

Exchanges such as this took place every evening. I had no understanding of the reason for them and found them exasperating. My father gave my mother the bulk of his weekly earnings every Thursday night, and referred to this as 'her wages'. The sum agreed with my mother was for the housekeeping, our clothing and her luxuries (lipstick, film money and her Gold Flake, into which he dipped without offering a refund). At the same time, the debts for the previous week were settled. My father took care of the utilities and his own tipple money. If he had to pay for a household item, he insisted on being refunded; likewise, if she paid the coalman, my father had to reimburse her. Today, I realise how liberated their thinking was.

He never encouraged her to drive. He offered to teach her, or have her taught, but in his heart he didn't really want her to. She sensed this, and never took the offer seriously. However, she insisted on being driven to the Novena, or to bingo, no matter how comfortably my father had settled himself in his armchair. As they'd be about to go out the door, she'd say,

'Wait there a minute, Johnny, 'til I spend a penny.'

'The divil shoot you, Mary,' he'd say.

I lived at home until I was eighteen and during that time my parents' relationship was as solid and permanent as the roof over my head. I never thought of them parting or having affairs, and I suspect that they never did. They squabbled and skirmished. He was apt to carelessly dig out her flowers and fork them into the barrow.

'Jesus, Johnny, did you dig up my chrysanths?'

'What chrysanths are you talking about?'

These disagreements were part of the daily fabric, and I saw them as normal. Singing was normal too. My father loved to bathe his feet in a milky Dettol mix and sing from a little black book of songs, written in his own hand. He preferred to do this beside the fire. He rolled up the legs of his pants, placed his feet in the basin, and began with 'The Emigrant's Letter':

'Dear Danny, I'm taking the pen in me hand
To tell you we're just out of sight of the land
In the grand Allem Liner I'm sailing in style
But I'm sailing away from the Emerald Isle.'

My mother sang too. She was happiest singing while doing the ironing. Sometimes they sang together. Their party piece was a morbid dirge called 'Kitty Wells', which they sang in harmony, until my mother complained that she no longer had the breath.

They were interdependent cogs, loving each other in their own way, for better or worse, until death. In 1991 they bowed out together.

Dave and I drove to Limerick to see my father, who by now was out of intensive care, singing the nurses' praises and admiring their behinds. What's more, he was no longer keeping his lustful thoughts to himself. My mother's sister, Margaret, had been summoned from England and accompanied her on a visit to his bedside that morning. As one of the duty nurses was leaving the ward, having taken his pulse, he informed his visitors that he thought that 'she'd be a great ride.'

'Sure he doesn't know what he's saying, God help us.'

'He doesn't, God knows.'

Margaret brought the story home and related it amusingly to all, with the comment:

'Well, he's not dead yet, anyway.'

'I hope he doesn't say anything like that in front of the priest,' said my mother.

'Maybe he'll tell the nurse to her face,' said Margaret, impishly.

'But she'll know he's not himself,' my mother pleaded.

When my father's condition stabilised enough to leave the hospital, he came home to spend another two and a half years in the armchair. His time was up, but he wasn't allowed to die. He now lived his life in a kind of limbo. He became frantic if my mother occupied the bathroom for more than five minutes at a time, being convinced that 'he'd destroy himself' if he didn't have access. He spent his days drifting in and out of sleep. When he found enough energy to move about, he would check the windows and lock my mother out of the house if she went to get a bucket of coal. It was disturbing to watch this fireball thrown in the armchair like a rag doll. I would have preferred him dead at this stage, with my memories still intact of his singing 'Thora' or 'Macushla', and his feet submerged in the Dettol mix.

His final call came on 27 June 1991. This time he was in the Regional Hospital, and again we were all summoned. I drove my mother and Margaret to the hospital and we sat for an hour watching his tortured departure. I had no experience of watching people dying and was unaware that we were witnessing his final hours. My mother, having been at many a bedside, was convinced that he was now unconscious, and eventually rang the emergency bell. A young intern arrived and immediately ushered us from the bedside to an adjoining room, while he assembled a team to try and return my father to the hell that he was trying to leave. Twenty minutes later he came to the room and announced that they'd lost him.

'I'm sorry, Mrs Hanly, we did our best. The nurse here will look after you, and Father O'Brien will be around shortly.'

We stood in the corridor, dumbstruck. After a lifetime in our company, my father had died alone.

When we re-entered the ward, he was already yellow and still, so still that I could no longer hold back my tears. As my eyes watered, his face became blurred, now clear, now blurred again. I gazed for an eternity wondering where this huge presence in my life had gone. I had no answers.

We drove back to St Patrick's Road, shattered. Despite all the warnings, his leaving was a shock. We mouthed comforts to each other.

'It's an ease to him, God help us, he was very agitated.'

'God be good to him, he was a good man.'

'Wouldn't you think that he'd have called us in, all the same?'

'Sure he was only a boy, Mary, that doctor.'

I called the plethora of cousins and friends, and the house was quickly teeming with sympathisers.

'He went quick in the end.'

'He was a beautiful singer, God bless him.'

'Are you in Dublin all the time, Mick?'

I poured myself a large glass of whiskey and settled into the task of being host.

'Can I get you something?' I asked my cousin, John Martin Dillon.

'Sure, whatever is there, Mick. He had no pain?'

'No, he was unconscious.'

'They don't let you die in pain any more. That's all done away with, and only right too.'

My mother sat in her armchair, complaining of a dryness in her mouth.

'What will I get you, Mam?'

'A glass of water, Michael, will be fine.'

As I was coming back with the glass of water, John Martin took my arm and said,

'I think your mother is having a bit of a turn, Mick.'

'Are you alright, Mam?' I asked.

She wasn't able to answer me. When she tried she became incoherent. All she could mutter was, 'Oh Jesus, oh Jesus'.

My mother was having an aneurysm, while sitting in the chair. She tried to get to her feet and make sense of her surroundings, but she sank back unsteadily.

'Stay where you are, Mary. It's the shock, God help us.'

We called an ambulance, and two hours after my father's body had been moved to the morgue, my mother arrived at the emergency doors of the same hospital. She survived for ten weeks. She missed my father's funeral, and had only a vague grasp of what was happening, who we were, or where she was. She was to mouth the phrase 'Oh Jesus, oh Jesus' ten thousand times before she died on 25 September 1991.

In the intervening ten weeks, my wife Marie's father, Mick,

died. As we trailed my mother's coffin, we were numb from funeral fatigue. It was an easy day's work for the grave-diggers as we laid her down forever on that rainy Saturday.

Hal Ketchum released his album, *Past the Point of Rescue*, in October 1991. Four months later he released the song itself as a single and it went to number two in the American Country Charts. It became BMI's most played Country song in the US in 1992, and Marie and I flew to London to pick up the award in The Dorchester.

The beautiful Ellen was born on 21 April 1992. She had all her fingers and all her toes, and her parents were overjoyed.

My ship had come in, but those I ached to share the news with were no longer there to take my call.

I Feel I Should Be Calling You

Verse 1

It's one whole year now since you left
Still the feeling of bereft
Hits me hard out of the blue
And I feel I should be calling you
With all this good news on my plate
Seems it came a year too late
It brought a smile surprised me too
And I feel I should be calling you.

Verse 2

The baby came and I was there
She has all her limbs but not a hair
Excuse me while I doff my hat
But I think I had a hand in that
On Mondays she's got her mother's eyes
On Tuesdays it's a compromise
On Wednesdays she's like you know who
And I feel I should be calling you.

Chorus

I feel I should be calling you
Sometimes the telephone is in my hand
Then I realise anew
That there's no-one there at all
There's no footstep in the hall
It's a silence that's so hard to understand.

Verse 3

The song went racing up the charts
Now that would have gladdened both your hearts
'Up The Pike' say all of us
Every day's like Christmas
So we threw a party and we hit the juice
You know the form the least excuse
It's sitting now at number two
And I feel I should be calling you.

Addend

I meet your friends on Mulgrave Street
They move along on weary feet
They knew you so they know me too
And I feel I should be calling you.

My parents, Mary and John,
on their wedding day, 1940

Sitting pretty? Kilkee 1950

Dad, David, Mam (back); me, Noel, Dolores (front). Kilkee 1950

Dad, Anne in arms, Dolores, David (back); Mam, Noel, me (front). Sunny days in St Patrick's Road, Limerick

Damaged Halo

For me the fear of school was as constant as a toothache. I could just about bear it, but it spoiled all my fun. The sense of relief which I felt on Fridays at three o'clock leaving the primary school, quickly turned to a sense of foreboding on Saturday evenings. Sunday — Mass day, good clothes day, English composition day — wasn't really a free day, but the countdown to another fear-filled unhappy week. In secondary school, every Saturday was stolen by obligatory school attendance until one o'clock, then afternoon training, or a match with the Dean Ryan and Harty hurling teams. The whole business filled me with such a sense of being dealt a bad hand that I swore I would never compel a child of mine to go to Saturday school. Today as my daughter Ellen is preparing to go to secondary, my promise to her is causing me an illogical dilemma. Illogical, because Ellen actually likes school. She is praised for her brightness, lauded for her answers, and proud of her achievements to date. She also shows no fear. But a promise is a promise, and since she gets to ride Topper, her favourite pony, on Saturday mornings, I reckon that I have a reasoned debate on my hands.

I started school in 1954, in St John's Convent, Limerick. I was a reluctant starter. I ran out the school gate the first chance I got and negotiated the uncharted mile home to St Patrick's Road. From that day on I was a marked man. The dark and wizened Sister Berchmans made sure that I never attempted the like again. Sister Mary Stapleton was my harbour in strange waters for the next few months but then she disappeared from my life, much to my consternation, for the next 40 years, only to turn up again when she wrote a letter to my brother David in 1996:

'Thanks again for coming to our defence at a time when the whole congregation is being tarred by the ill-advised actions of a few, and by the way, tell your brother Michael that I taught him briefly when he went to St John's Convent.'

'Could this be the beautiful grown-up who used to laugh when I imitated the way she counted the class in twos with the two fingers of her right hand?' I wrote. 'Yes, I am the nun who used to count . . . .' We met recently in the University Concert Hall in Limerick. Her two nieces brought her along and introduced her to me after the show. I told her that she was the first woman with whom I'd ever fallen in love, and she admonished me by rapping me on the arm with her rolled-up programme. 'But you were the brightest boy in the class,' she added impishly. She hasn't lost her sense of fun, or charm.

Sister Laurence was benign and fair, and made sure that I had a banana on my tray when we went picnicking on the grassy lawn of the priests' house beside St John's Cathedral.

We were a ragbag collection of children. I look at the photograph today of the 39 boys and the rocking horse that was used to lure me into the classroom, and I can still remember most of them by name. I can pick out the lads who came to school in wellingtons and no socks in winter. I can pick out the lads who smelled, the lads whose bowel or bladder let them down. I can count on the fingers of one hand the number that went to the Christian Brothers' secondary school and on the fingers of two the number that I ever saw again.

Every now and then Jackie Tynne (who was my mother's uncle and whom we all called Uncle Jackie) would ask me 'what book' I was in and had me warned that, when the Brothers got their hands on me, I could look out for squalls. He wasn't the only one who talked of the Brothers in such terms. It seemed to me that everyone was intent on expressing their own private glee at the fact that they'd done their stint and now it was my turn to face the music. Sister Berchmans taught my own mother, and I heard my mother say that 'she was an awful *divil* in my time as well.' If my mother was prepared to allow a crusty old crab-apple like Sister Berchmans loose on me, then I had to accept that she would be prepared to allow the widely-rumoured crazy Christian Brothers loose on me too. She had already done so to my older brothers, David and Noel, and Michael was the next for the high jump.

All predictions were to prove true. On the first day of primary, we were marched into the classroom of a man called Warty Monaghan. His name was John, but had a small black growth on his right cheek so he was christened Warty, and Warty he was forever. The first thing that Warty did was produce the rung of a chair and without warning brought it crashing down on Timmy Cantelon's desk. Timmy jumped a foot out of his desk with the fright and the rest of us got the message.

In Second Class we had the doddery Brother Timmons, whose leather was so worn it was like a rubber wand. He used the rubber wand liberally on our legs when we strayed outside the pink lines of our *scríobhnóireacht* copies. Every morning, late arrivers had to face the cold wrath of Brother King or 'Kingo' as he was known.

'My mother had to go to hospital, Sir!'

'Hospital, is it, I'll give you hospital, me bucko.' Kingo's leather was not rubbery and stung like hell in the winter chill. What a wonderful way for a young boy to begin his love of learning.

A lifetime later a very drunken man approached me after a gig in Ennistymon and told me that he had something for me. After gigs, I usually give people who say that they have something for me a wide berth. When they're pissed I add an extra yard. This man persisted, and when I consented to listen to what he had to say, he gave me a Christian Brother's leather. 'I've been keeping that for you,' he said. How and where he got the leather I couldn't get out of him, but I have the leather at home. I can only think that he was a Christian Brother himself and wasn't prepared to own up. Or else he had taken on a mission to steal the leather from some Brother and, as a result of the post-traumatic stress suffered, he became an alcoholic.

There was the benign Mr Horan, in Third Class. I could tell by his body language that he didn't particularly like using the stick, but use it he did when he felt that the message wasn't getting through. It was in Mr Horan's class that I first stood in front of an audience, seeking applause. It was hard-won, but it was worth it and it planted the seed for my future escape. He called for a class concert and asked us all to prepare something for it. Mr Horan promptly forgot about this, but Stephen Benson and I took his request very seriously. Stephen, who was well on his way to being a full-blown gay person, or maybe I should say he was doing well in his gay apprenticeship, recited a poem called, prophetically enough,

'Fairies in the Bathroom'. I sang 'Living Doll'. I was determined to add some extras, which turned the rendering of the
songs into a 'holy show' and embarrassed me at the time, but
in hindsight it's easy to see that making a 'holy show' was
what I intended to do with my life.

A few days before the concert, my mother found me busy
with cardboard, scissors, biro and lengths of fishing gut,
trying to make myself a guitar. I cut out a passable imitation,
which bent on the original box crease. I drew a sound-hole on
the cut-out, and tied some pieces of gut across it. It didn't
make a sound and bent like doddery Timmons's rubber leather.
I wasn't making much of an impression, even on my mother,
so she suggested that I borrow her Kilkee hat. This was the
straw hat which she brought to the seaside resort of Kilkee,
Co. Clare, every summer. It was a hat which offered protection
from the sun: my mother was ever the optimist. I decided that
I might as well be hung for a sheep as a lamb and tied one of
her scarves round my neck, Gene Autrey style. Whatever about
my singing, my wardrobe was certainly going to impress. If I
could have been magically transported, there and then, from
my bedroom to the bright lights of Third Class, the whole
episode would have been relatively painless, but it wasn't to be.

On concert day, I packed my stage clothes in a pillowcase
and ran the gauntlet of the teeming schoolyard.

'Whass in de bag? Gis a look, gis a look.'

'A guitar.'

'Das norra guitar, you eejit, das owney carboard.'

As I said, Mr Horan had forgotten that he'd ever called for
a concert, but the class, who would burn their own mothers
at the stake for diversion, weren't long about reminding him.

'Warrabout the concert, Sir?'

'*Ciúnas.*'

'Sir, Sir, Hanly has a guitar, Sir.'

'Hanly, *suas leat*. What are those *pleidhces** talking about?'

'You said we were having a concert today, Sir. I have a guitar, Sir.'

'Geetar! Well *taispeáin dúinn an geetar, a Hanly bhocht.*'

I pulled my bent instrument from the pillowcase. This was greeted with howls of laughter.

'*Ciúnas*, let ye. *Agus an bhfuil tú ábalta an geetar a sheint, Hanly, a mhic?*'

'I dunno, Sir. I made it, Sir.'

'Well, *suas leat agus abair amhrán dúinn.*'

'Sir, Sir, Sir, he has a hat too, Sir.'

'I don't want to bother with the hat, Sir.'

'*Ná bí ag imirt pleidhce, Hanly. Suas leat agus cuir do hata ort.*'

The blue and white straw hat drew more howls from the audience. My mother's scarf came out of the pillowcase with the hat, and whoever was in the desk next to me grabbed it and threw it over my shoulders. They were determined to get their full ten bob's worth.

I went to the top of the class and Mr Horan went to the side wall to be part of the audience. My inquisitors were foaming at the mouth as the flames licked my feet. I dropped the second chorus of 'Living Doll' and the moves that I'd practised in front of my bedroom mirror. But after a verse of burning at the stake, I became the defiant heretic, and insisted on doing two songs. The response to my first performance was delirious and way over the top. I knew it for what it was because I'd been a willing mob participant myself on many an occasion. Still, it was approval. It was applause. It was reward for stepping outside the loop. I went for a cowboy song with

* Irish: *pleidhce* = a fool

a newly-found gusto. Mr Horan was hugely amused. The response was more overwhelming than before.

'*Ciúnas, ciúnas*, let ye. *Maith a' fear, Hanly.*'

I sat down with pleasure coursing through my veins. Stephen did 'Fairies in the Bathroom' to renewed howls, and, though I thought that mine was the better act, I had a suspicion that he received a bigger round of applause. Going home was an anticlimax. Nobody was interested in the pillowcase any more and no-one mentioned my performance.

'Well, how did the concert go?' my mother asked.

'T'was awright.'

'And did they like your hat?'

'I dunno.'

Fourth and Fifth Classes were a sort of limbo where we languished until we were delivered into the hands of the big hitters, Brothers Farrell and Ó Hora. I used to watch them in trepidation as they strode through the host in their dusty soutanes, cross-faced, hands clasped behind their backs, cutting a swathe, no doubt discussing who was getting uppity and who was not delivering on their potential. Nothing that a few flakes of a leather wouldn't cure.

From the two years in Fourth and Fifth a few memories stand out. One of the teachers, Mr Gilligan, was beating a boy with such force that the stick he was using broke, and a splinter flew into Gilligan's eye. He lost the sight of his eye and there was silent cheering all round. In Fifth Class, Mr Ahern stood in front of us with a book on the *Facts of Life* in his hand. His face went scarlet as he told us what the real name for our 'mickey' was. This produced howls of laughter and the class became ungovernable. Naturally, he never got to the word 'clitoris'.

One day, Ger O'Malley was pretending that the seven-foot window pole was a lance. Unfortunately, the lance flew out of Ger's hand and straight through a pane of glass in the class partition. His offence was so grave that he was sent upstairs to the big hitters. He came back red-eyed and wasn't able to hold a lance for a couple of weeks.

There were five different streams in Sixth Class. There were 6a, b, c, d and 6x. The six-exers were the scholarship class. We were expected to shine and spare our parents the cost of our secondary education. My brother David, my sister Anne and I got scholarships, and the precious few pounds were always earmarked by my mother to take care of some bill or other. In 6x I shared my desk with a guy called 'Ducky' Ryan. 'Ducky' had a nervous kind of smile, which was often mistaken for a smirk by Farrell and Ó Hora. He was constantly being told to wipe it off his face and sometimes he was hammered for not realising that he was wearing it. I liked 'Ducky' a lot and I wrote a song about him called 'Birthmark' for my *All I Remember* album, but I didn't welcome the attention that he attracted. That said, we were as close as two kids from different parts of the city could be and stoically took our hidings together.

We were some weeks into our first term in 6x when, one day, Ó Hora was told that there was a woman at the classroom door to see him.

'Who is it, Browne?'

'A woman, Sir.'

'Did you ask the woman what she wanted, Browne?'

Browne went to the door again to make sure of his facts.

'She said she wants to talk to you, Sir.'

Ó Hora flung the piece of chalk that he was using into the well of the blackboard.

'*Ar aghaidh libh le teoirim a cúig.* I'll expect ye to have it off by heart by the time I get back.'

Most Christian Brothers were uncomfortable in the presence of women and Ó Hora was no exception. Luckily for Ó Hora and his fellow brothers, women rarely showed their faces in Sexton Street, unless goaded into action by the barbarity of a beating their boy had received.

The woman at the door was Mrs Grace. Her son Timmy was in 6d, the class for academic lost causes, most of whom became car dealers, builders and small business people. They would later drive Ford Granadas, while those in 6x, who became bankers, ESB clerks and civil servants, were saving up for their Morris 1100s. Timmy had jumped on the train from Limerick to Dublin on Saturday morning and gone missing for a couple of days before hunger made him jump on the Dublin-to-Limerick train and return home.

The demented Mrs Grace was at her wit's end and came to one of the heavy hitters to sort Timmy out. We could hear her pleading with Ó Hora at the door. We could hear his own indignation at the dastardliness of Timmy's behaviour and his reassurances that the lesson, which Timmy so urgently needed, was about to be taught. When Mrs Grace finally left, Ó Hora came into the classroom, disgruntled, impatient and baying for blood. He silently wrote four mathematical problems on the blackboard and allowed his own blood to boil. He then took a brand new, golden leather from a locked drawer in his desk. It was crisp and still velvety at the edges. It was stiff, barely more pliable than a piece of two-by-one, and was about to be given its first field test. He slid the weapon into the deep pocket of his soutane.

'Browne, go down to Mr McCormack and tell him to send Timmy Grace up to Brother Ó Hora.'

'Where, Sir?'

'In 6d, you *amadán*, do you not know where Mr McCormack is?'

'I do, Sir.'

'Well, *brostaigh ort.*'

Browne came back and a minute later there was a knock on the door. By now the class was in a state of high anxiety, knowing a storm was about to break.

'*Tar isteach.*'

Grace entered the classroom with a look on his face that was familiar to us all. It was a mixture of terror and denial. Timmy had been in trouble so often that lying came more easily to him than telling the truth. He was now about to deny everything, and bring even more wrath on his young shoulders.

'Ah, the journeyman. Fancy being a bit of a hobo, do you, Grace?'

Timmy didn't know what the word hobo meant, but he guessed it was derogatory, so he chanced a 'no' in reply.

'No, no, well now, I heard that you were a great man for the tracks.'

'I don't know, Sir.'

By now Grace was twitching nervously. Ó Hora was using a tactic much favoured by teachers of the time. Confuse and humiliate the victim by talking above his head and using language that was unfamiliar to him, then hang the victim out to dry with the slow release of information that he doesn't know you have.

'And where did you go to Mass on Sunday, Mr Grace?'

'In Janesboro, Sir.'

'Oh, in Janesboro, you say. Would that be Janesboro in Limerick or would that be Janesboro in Dublin, by any chance?'

Grace began to shift like a trapped animal.

'In Limerick, Sir.'

'In Limerick, you say, and did you say a prayer to St Christopher, tell me?'

Grace chanced a 'yes'.

'You did. I thought you might. St Christopher is the patron saint of all travellers, did you know that?'

'No, Sir.'

'But you prayed to him all the same.'

'I did, Sir.'

'Good man. I'll tell you now what you'll do, Mr Grace. You can go back outside the door and wait until I'm ready for you. I need to teach you a thing or two about your prayers and your saints.'

Grace was left to ponder his fate for the next five minutes while Ó Hora sat silently menacing the class. When the storm broke it was worse than our worst imaginings. Ó Hora left the classroom and the assault took place in the corridor outside the classroom door. There was a thumping session accompanied by squeals of denial.

'Where did you go to Mass, you tyke?'

'Janesboro, Sir.'

'Lies, Grace, more lies.'

The classroom door was six inches ajar. Suddenly it slammed shut having been hit by Grace's body. Browne mustered up the courage to run to the keyhole and run back again, showing nerve I hadn't given him credit for before.

'He's getting pasted,' he announced. The assault went on for longer than our own thumping hearts could bear. We felt sorry for Grace, but we resented the fact that he was delivering us into the hands of a raging, guilt-racked monster for the rest of the day. There was another three minutes of hysterical denials, blows, and finally tears and capitulation. Then the golden leather was produced. We could see it all in our mind's eye. We felt every stroke. We saw Grace's body contorting like a stuck worm, heard his 'Ahgodagodagods'. There was an awful dawning. This was what possibly awaited the boys of 6x for the rest of the year. The assault finally stopped when Ó Hora had exhausted himself. Timmy Grace didn't go on to secondary school and I never saw or heard of him again.

Gabey Tobin was a small, gutsy survivor in the schoolyard, in the classroom and in the Brothers' Field. (The Brothers' Field was where we played all our school sports. It was about a mile and a half from the school, and had but the most meagre of facilities. It was only when we went to play hurling matches against schools such as Roscrea College, which was a fee-paying boarding school, that we understood at what end of the social spectrum CBS Limerick lay.) Gabey was picked on a lot because of his size but he never lay down without a fight. I saw Gabey get mauled by bigger guys a couple of times, but the bigger guys always ended up with some reminder of Gabey's fighting spirit — a throbbing pair of balls, where Gabey had landed a sneaky kick, a bite on an arm, a chunk of hair out of their heads. They weren't too quick to tangle with such a porcupine again, but compared to Gabey, there were lots of big guys.

'Tháinig Long Ó Valparaiso' was Gabey's Irish poem. The sallow-faced Brother Farrell, who taught us Irish, English, Geography and Religion, gave everyone in the class an Irish poem to learn. The only morsel of poetry that I can remember from this particular exercise is Gabey Tobin's 'Tháinig Long Ó Valparaiso' and the reason I do is as follows.

Farrell was a smirker. He delighted in humiliating pupils and he engendered respect through fear. For spontaneous punishment Farrell drew his leather from the pocket of his soutane like a six-gun. For ritual punishment he used the hurley across the behind. I remember one weekend spending at least two hours of 'cowboys and indians' playtime working on an essay. I tried to let my imagination fly. On the following Tuesday morning he threw the essay on my desk and asked me did I think that I was 'some class of smart Alec or what'?

The punishment for not knowing your Irish poem (for 'not knowing' read delaying too long to recollect your thoughts) was ritual. You were sent to the line to await your punishment with the rest of the condemned. Of course the wait was far worse than the actual blow, and the blow that I was about to receive was complicated by the fact that I had a patch on my pants, which caused me huge embarrassment. Some of the boys were already wearing long pants and I was having a battle trying to persuade my mother to let me do likewise. But she was thrifty and prudent, and my brother Noel's confirmation suit had not gotten the wear that she would have deemed to be value for money. What's more, he had managed to decorate the pants with a perfect right-angled, cat-wire tear, and the repaired short pair of pants was passed on to me. A seamstress friend of my mother's had done a wonderful job and had fitted the pants with a completely new seat, but back then I was unable to appreciate the delicacy of her work.

Gabey never made it past the first line of '*Tháinig Long Ó Valparaiso*'. He was so frozen with fear that it stuck in his throat like a dobber.

'*Amach leat, a leanbh.*'

And so the cultivation of our love for the language and poetry continued. Having had numerous confidence-boosting sojourns at the line throughout the year, Gabey didn't get a scholarship and disappeared from my life when we broke up for summer holidays. I went on to complete secondary school, getting a five-honours Inter Cert and Leaving Cert along the way. It wasn't without its heartache.

In First Year secondary, a young thug, just out of seminary, brought tears to my eyes in front of the class because I'd spelled the word 'Gaeilge' wrongly on the cover of my Irish composition copy. He repeatedly struck me across the face with his open hand. The next time I saw that kind of treatment being meted out was in Nazi war films. The hurt was magnified by the fact that I was captain of the class hurling team, and I was so conditioned by the corporal punishment system that I was afraid to defend myself.

In Fifth Year secondary, we had a long streak of misery of an Irish lay teacher, whose idea of imbuing us with a love of the native tongue was to lift those who were slow with their *gramadach* from their desks by the hair.

There were also exceptions. In Second and Third Year, I was taught most subjects by Brother Mullane. He was a decent man and an enthusiastic teacher. He was also fair. The corporal punishment regime was abused by many of the teachers who used it to victimise and humiliate youngsters that they didn't like. Brother Mullane never did. He packed a leather, like the rest, but he used it judiciously. I picked up on his enthusiasm, and worked hard for his approval.

In Fifth and Sixth Year, our main teacher was Brother Keating. He was also the trainer of the Harty Cup hurling team, of which I was a member. Consequently, most of my academic shortcomings were forgiven, and my constant late arrivals to class in the mornings were overlooked. The hurling team reached the All-Ireland Colleges final in 1967 and we played St Peter's of Wexford in Birr. It ended in a draw, and the replay was held in Croke Park. My only memory of the game is a dent in my shin which was left there by John Quigley.

As a consequence of the long campaign, I was well behind academically. Brother Keating (or Sammy as he was known to us students) gave up his Sunday mornings to give me private tuition, in Maths, Maths Physics and Physics. I returned the compliment by getting honours in all three subjects. He was a wonderful and generous man. He is now in his seventy-ninth year. I had the pleasure of meeting him recently and discovered for the first time that his name is Michael.

Jack Costelloe (bass player with the band Grannies Intentions) was not so lucky. His 'Small Faces'-type hairstyle, and his fierce independence, were mocked and resented by all the teachers. Three months before the Leaving Cert examination, Jack left school and threw in his lot with the 'Grannies', amongst whom his hairstyle was cool, and his independence was regarded as good-humoured rebellion. He now runs a successful business in London, and I doubt if he ever returned to sit the Leaving Cert.

Twelve months ago, I was playing in a bar in Limerick. During the gig I noticed a small guy standing by the wall. I switched to autopilot while my mind trawled my back pages. By the end of the song I'd put Gabey's name on the face and my stomach started to churn, even at 40 years' remove, from the memory of the smirker Farrell and his hurley. During the interval I went straight to Gabey.

'How's the going, Gabey?'

'Jesus Christ, you don't remember me, Mick, do you?'

'Course I do. You're Gabey Tobin, aren't you? *Tháinig Long Ó Valparaiso*.'

'Jesus Christ, that's a good one.'

We hadn't seen each other for so many years, yet it was as though we were talking outside the school gates. He recalled former classmates and their subsequent histories, stopping now and then to ask, 'Do you remember Tony-This or Jimmy-That?'

'Are you in Dublin all the time?'

I explained that I'd moved to Thomastown in Kilkenny, and had been living there for the last thirteen years.

'You'll hardly come home at this stage?' For Gabey, Limerick was home to anyone who'd been born there, no matter how long their absence.

'But what about yourself?' I asked.

'Me? I went to the Tech, Mick, an' I became a fitter. I went into CIE and they made a foreman of me. I've done okay, Mick.'

'That's terrific,' I said.

'And wait'll I tell you, didn't I have a stroke of luck.'

'What d'you mean?'

'I won the Lotto.'

Damaged Halo

Verse 1
Why would a clever boy leave school with a star
And walk out through the gates feeling worthless
Put the pennies that he's saved on a cheap sunburst guitar
Work his fingers to the bone to be noticed.

Verse 2
Why would a clever boy take his school books and abscond
With his fear around his neck like a damaged halo
Be hounded out the door 'cause he couldn't get beyond
The first line of *Tháinig Long Ó Valparaiso*.

Chorus
Look at me, look at me
I can play, I can play
Look at me, am I not worth lovin'?
Look at me, look at me
I can play, I can play
'The Forty Shades of Green' and some Slim Whitman.

Verse 3
Why would a clever boy when all is said and done
Turn to every bauble stick become addicted
Tongue-tied, sad and blue, forever on the run
Like a poor beast in the rain too blind to fix it.

Verse 4

We were damaged by the score, the clever and the dumb
With our scars were shunted into every siding
For the voiceless there are tears and a million more to come
Will you tell me where in Christ was Jesus hiding?

Chorus

Verse 5

Here's a postscript to make you smile, you know my *Valparaiso*
    friend
For years I wondered how he wore that halo
He was apprenticed, did his time, climbed the ladder in the
    end
Then one day he pulled a ticket in the Lotto.

'Lured by the rocking-horse'. St John's Convent 1954/55. Me second row from top, extreme left

Limerick CBS Harty Cup winners, 1967. (left to right) Back row: Matt Grace (Old Christians), Pat Hartigan (South Liberties), Sean Foley (Patrickswell), Sean Bourke (Garryspillane), Gerry McKeown, Ritchie Grade RIP, Willie O'Connor and Al Flannery (all Old Christians). Front row: Christy Campbell, me and Dave Toughy (all Old Christians), Tony Fitzgerald (Treaty Sarsfields), Pat McCarthy (Caherline) (captain), John Condon (Fedamore) and Liam Moynihan (Old Christians)

Christian Brothers,
St. Michael's Place,
Limerick.

Mainistir na mBráithre,
Plás San Micheál,
Luimneach.

AINM ... M. Hanley.

Rang. 3ú Bl. .... Téarma (Term). Nollaig '66

Pas (Pass) 40		Onóracha (Honours) 60	
	Samhain '66	Nollaig '66	
Eolas Diaga (Religion)	—	79	per cent.
Gaeilge (Irish)	70	43	,, ,,
English	61	47	,, ,,
Laidin (Latin)	69	47	,, ,,
Fraincis (French)	28	44	,, ,,
Stair (History)	{ 61	21 — ,, v. weak
Tíreolaíocht (Geography)	—	70	,, ,,
Uimhríocht (Arithmetic)	77	60	,, ,,
Ailgéabar (Algebra)	62	65	,, ,,
Céimseata (Geometry)	80	35 — ,, v. weak
Tráchtáil (Commerce)	—	—	,, ,,
Mat. Fheidhm (App. Maths.)	—	—	,, ,,
Eolaíocht (Science)	—	41 — ,, weak.
Fisic (Physics)			,, ,,
Ceimic (Chemistry)			,, ,,
Toradh (Result)			,, ,,

Nótaí ar obair an Téarma . (Remarks on work and progress)

General conduct satisfactory.
Michael is capable of doing much better.
He appears to have too many distractions.

Athoscailt na Scoile (School repens) ...11th. Jan.

Br. Mullane
Superior .... Uachtarán

Another report will be forwarded at Easter.

Too busy playing the guitar!

Christian Brothers,
St. Michael's Place,
Limerick.

Mainistir na mBráithre,
Plás San Micheál,
Luimneach.

AINM Miceál Ó hAnlaí

Rang. 1A1 .... Téarma (Term). 1st

Pas (Pass) 40	Onóracha (Honours) 60	
Eolas Diaga (Religion)	40	per cent.
Gaeilge (Irish)	67	,, ,,
English	79	,, ,,
Laidin (Latin)	70	,, ,,
Fraincis (French)	40	,, ,,
Stair (History)	76	,, ,,
Tíreolaíocht (Geography)	74	,, ,,
Uimhríocht (Arithmetic)	95	,, ,,
Ailgéabar (Algebra)	67	,, ,,
Céimseata (Geometry)	74	,, ,,
Tráchtáil (Commerce)	—	,, ,,
Mat. Fheidhm (App. Maths.)		,, ,,
Eolaíocht (Science)	78	,, ,,
Fisic (Physics)		,, ,,
Ceimic (Chemistry)	Elocution 50	,,
Toradh (Result)	Onóracha	,,

Nótaí ar obair an Téarma . (Remarks on work and progress)

Conduct excellent, lazy at work
would need to spend more time
at exercises especially memorising

Athoscailt na Scoile (School repens) 9th January

S Sármhaith ...... Uachtarán
Superior

DUST IN THE STORM

I came across the following quote in the letters page of *The Irish Times* recently: 'Why, we must wonder, would the shaper of the Universe have frittered away 13 billion years, turning out quadrillions of useless stars, before getting around to the one thing he really cared about, seeing to it that a miniscule minority of earthling vertebrates are washed clean of sin and guaranteed an eternal place in his company.'

The quote was attributed to a Professor Frederick Crews. On foot of this I went to the Internet to find out who Professor Crews was, and whence the quote. I found a Berkeley professor by the same name who works on the lives of invertebrates, and other forms of lowlife not involved in the music business. I couldn't confirm the quote, though I did write to the letter-writer without reply. To some, this kind of scientific rationalisation is very thin and unsatisfying gruel; to me, it makes a lot of sense.

I look up at the sky every morning on my way to work in my studio. Sometimes it's clear, more often it's featureless navy. On the clear mornings I look at the stars, while 'Pepper' the Jack Russell is doing his business (he takes a long time to choose a depository area and shape himself for the deed). I regard this stargazing as a privilege, and one of the perks of living in the countryside. However, before too long I'm overwhelmed. Trying to place the earth in this maelstrom confounds me. Trying to imagine that the galaxy, of which the earth is but a particle, is itself but a puff of dust in the great storm leaves me floundering. And all this is expanding at a colossal speed, into what? Into where? Into new space being created as I write? Where is the room for this? If that's not baffling enough, trying to place myself, and my helpless tinyness in this great confusion, or scheme, is futile. I cope by calling it 'the mystery', and I'm grateful to be part of it. I'm grateful when the sun rises in the morning and the moon lights my way at night; for my own good health and the good health of my family; and for the breaks and perks that I've been given in life. I also realise it's as fragile as a spider's web, and could crumble in a thrice.

Most of the time I'm happy to be overwhelmed. I'm happy to be overwhelmed by the exquisite beauty of a goldfinch pestering ragwort, or the trill of the wren's song. Every spring I feel like shedding tears of joy when I sight my first swallow of the new year, or notice the first rhubarb blister breasting the frost. These days, this feeling is tempered by a rueful sadness for the ticking of my own finite clock. The mystery moves me from sadness to joy a hundred times a day. Sometimes it leaves me crippled, mostly it exhilarates. Trying to balance the two is my day's work. I consider myself blessed to be a part of this simple and awesome pageant. If I didn't have to pay the electricity bill, I'd happily gaze at a purling stream for all my waking hours.

I accept the random cruelty and beauty of all natural things, but I have no explanations. When Ellen and Katie demand to know why the unblinking mink snaps up an adorable gosling and takes the fluffy, cheeping snack back to its equally adorable *minkettes* to be torn to shreds, I don't have an acceptable answer.

'That's lousy,' they say.

I agree. I want to say, 'It is lousy, but that's the way the cookie crumbles'; 'Life's a bitch'; 'It's God's holy will.'

I prefer to say nothing because none of these answers make sense to a ten-year-old. If I'm pressed I say, 'I don't know.'

The only way I can counter their horror at this random, year-round babyfest is to insist that they follow the progress of the survivors. I make sure that we visit the swallow's nest daily. We take photographs of every clutch and celebrate their first flight onto the nearest telephone wire. I warn them that the second clutch might be nature's mistake and that they might not have sufficient reserves to carry them to South Africa and back. If I find a blackbird's nest in the shrubbery, I keep the girls abreast of the family's progress, and part the brambles gingerly to allow them view the fluffy chicks. They go 'ahhh' and run off reassured. If a magpie devours them all in one raid, I tell them that they've successfully flown the coop. Lies. White, positive lies.

I understand the benign or withering rays of the sun. I understand the comfort of the blue lagoon and the fear of the ocean's fury; the mercilessness of the desert and the indifference of the freezing sea. Scratch the surface and I'm as frightened as a Neanderthal.

Nevertheless, I have difficulty with the concept of God. I have particular difficulty with the relatively recent phenomenon of conferring godhood on holy men. I'm most comfortable with the concept of elemental gods. But I can understand the reasons for man-made gods, and respect the fact that they

provide solace for millions. I'm also well aware that to deny the
existence of God is deeply sacrilegious in the minds of many,
and I can't change that. Far wiser men than I have concluded
that there is a benign architect, and I respect their wisdom. I
respect their endless searching, and their conclusions. All I ask
in turn is their respect for my choice to do my own searching,
and come to my own conclusions.

I appreciate the need for ritual and continuity in the face
of the unexpected flood or pestilence, and the simple trials of
life. The simple trials of life are not simple. Were Ellen or
Katie to be diagnosed with leukaemia in the morning, I don't
know how I'd cope. Were my stepson, Thomas, now an
American Marine, to be blown up by a roadside bomb in Iraq,
I don't know how Marie and I would recover. My agnosticism
has never been really tested by life's cruel vagaries.

I was brought up a Roman Catholic. Before my father got
his first car we were sent to St John's Cathederal to eight
o'clock Mass every morning, and not being all that interested,
I often found myself alone in the schoolyard while the care-
taker went about her chores. Sometimes I detoured through
Garryowen, searching for birds' nests, or wheels, or hoops, or
anything that might come in useful for my stockpile of
reusable rubbish which I kept at home under the privet hedge.
When my father got his first Morris Minor, we were loaded
into the back of it and driven to the Augustinian Church, for
eight o'clock Mass, to receive Holy Communion, come home
and have breakfast before going to school. My mother stayed
home to cook the porridge and set the fire. She went later on
her bicycle to the Franciscan, and collected her Keane's loaf
and some meagre toiletries from Denis Moran's Hardware
Store. The Hanlys were a model Roman Catholic family. My
brothers and I were inducted into the boys' section of the

Arch Confraternity of the Holy Family and were ever-present under our father's watchful eye. We progressed from the Boys to the Junior Men, and ultimately to the Men. In the Boys the preacher told us stories about a hero called Dan Strong, which held us spellbound. When we graduated to the Junior Men the stories about Dan Strong were dropped and we had to listen to sermons, which left us scratching our heads and gazing at the intricacies of the church ceiling. We sang:

'Confraternity men to the fight,
Raise up your banners on high.'

We cycled from St Patrick's Road to Mount St Alphonsus's Church on dark mornings for the Mission. Our bicycle lamps were joined by an assortment of other lamps from different corners of the city as we responded to this unique Redemptorist trumpet. I remember a feeling of elation and purity from these excursions, and went to school feeling that I was a good boy, and that God and I had a special relationship. The senseless violent crack on the head for a blotted copybook threw these feelings into confusion.

In spite of this diligent foundation building by my parents, my so-called faith turned out to be a house of cards. I stopped going to Mass as soon as I could get away with it and never went back. Today, I attend funerals, weddings, christenings, etc., because I respect the beliefs of my neighbours and friends. I would prefer the Tridentine version and the old hymns, but that might be inverted nostalgia. When the details of the appalling Church scandals began to emerge in the 80s, I wrote to the parish priest in St Patrick's Church in Limerick and asked him to remove my name from the register. I no longer wanted to be officially listed in the ranks of the believers and used as a statistic to bolster the numbers of the 'overwhelming majority'. It was an angry and unreflective reaction, but I haven't rescinded it.

Today, I find the Christian version of the man-god particularly difficult, and baulk at the certainties on offer. I baulk at the certainties that all religions have to offer. I find the adherence to the certainties of sacred books and the waving of them in my face abhorrent. After 54 years on this beautiful and mysterious ball, my only certainty, apart from our own finiteness, is that there are no certainties. Nevertheless, I'm all too well aware of the power of simple faith, from observing the life of my maternal grandmother.

My grandmother was a beautiful human being. She was imbued with good sense, kindness, tolerance and good humour all her life. For her, every piece of ill-luck or good fortune was attributed to God's holy will. Sometimes, his Blessed Mother was also invoked.

'Thanks be to Jesus and his blessed Mother' was a salutation frequently and sincerely expressed.

She had a hard life. Her father was violent in drink, and her mother, as a buffer against his rages, kept her at home from school. Consequently, she never learned to read or write. By all accounts, she was a beautiful child and most of the time his tempers were assuaged by her being passed over to him, to dandle on his knee. It didn't always work, and once he beat her so badly that he was committed to St Joseph's Mental Hospital, never to emerge. He was 40 years old at the time. His insanity was being a 'martyr to the drink'. To add to the enormous sadness of this, the back wall of his cottage home in the Pike was also the perimeter wall of St Joseph's. He became a helper to the staff nurses. Being powerful and muscular himself, he helped with bathing the strongest and most reluctant patients. He could have left St Joseph's at any time but chose not to. Why he chose to remain in St Joseph's is a question that I can't answer. It was alluded to occasionally but never discussed in depth. Being a 'martyr to the drink' or 'He must have been a bit odd' doesn't explain spending 46 sane years among the insane, in the confines of St Joseph's. He died there in 1954, aged 86.

My grandmother's husband, Davy, died when he was 28. She was 21 at the time and never remarried. She was left with three children to rear — my mother Mary, Margaret her sister and their brother John. She believed that this was the cross that God had chosen for her and she bore it with fortitude. Other women were also burdened with crosses. Drunken, violent husbands, stillbirths, and consumption which galloped through the house and stole the treasured ones who had been born healthy. Respite and recovery was as a result of prayers offered, candles lit, and precious pennies offered for the holy sacrifice of the Mass. This outlook on life carried my grandmother and millions of others through their darkest hours. For millions, it still does.

I've thought a lot about the trials of my grandmother's life, and would forgive her if she had been as sour as a crab-apple; truth is she was one of the most serene and positive people that I've ever met. She could also be jolly. When my mother opened the sherry bottle to add a drop to the makings of the Christmas cake, she always offered my granny a small tipple. Not being a drinker, the smell of the alcohol immediately triggered my granny's dancing instincts. Before long she was sashaying round the kitchen table with whatever partner was to hand. Sometimes, it was myself, gauche and embarrassed, but that didn't bother her. Her *coup de grâce* was a daring lifting of her skirt to about two inches above the bottom gusset of her blue drawers.

'Now for ye,' she'd say, and resume her armchair, breathless.

Her unquestioning faith in Jesus Christ worked. She had the ability to gather all her trials into a basket and plant that basket straight back into his lap. Her humble acceptance of her own powerlessness made her powerful. To me, she was more convincing that a thousand gospel singers. There was never a better advertisement for unquestioning faith.

Yet, today I'm still at sea. Today, for me, organised religion is still beguiling hokum. Today, I'm still looking at the stars, aghast, fascinated, helpless and still searching.

Marie and I do our best to imbue our children with values and self-esteem. We don't believe that they were born with an original sin, so we didn't have to rectify that. As it happens, the chief tenet of our value system is a Christian one: 'love and respect your neighbour as you would love and respect yourself' with the caveat, 'don't turn the other cheek in the face of injustice.' Our children have no fear of the fury of devils or benign architects. They have no concept of hell or sin, but they do know the difference between right and wrong. (That is not to say that they don't have fears. They do and plenty of them, but they usually respond to reassurance.) They are loved and given plenty of that commodity which they cherish most — our time. Where possible, they are included in all of our comings and goings. But there are no guarantees. When the time comes for them to look at the stars, they may come up with a different answer. If the rock of our unconditional love is not strong enough, they may cry foul and declare that their lives are empty. This is risk that we have to take.

I don't like being told that there is only one, true way. When I observe the zealous behaviour of the purveyors of certainty, I detect a stronger-than-normal whiff of cordite. We find our dreams when nobody's beating on the drums. Now, where did I hear that before?

Dust in the Storm

Verse 1

Take a look at the stars for a moment if you have a moment
    to spare
I know life is short and it's so hard to squeeze in a moment
    somewhere
You might be the one at the window, or the soul in the desert
    wide-eyed
Believe me you're not all alone or the first to be beautifully
    mystified.

Verse 2

Lend an ear to the sound of the ocean if you want to hear
    more that the sea
Stay, there's nothing to fear at the door to eternity
Draw back the curtain forever, take a ride on a handful of dust
If you still think the good book's the answer go back to bed
    with that book if you must.

Chorus

But please let me find my own way, my own way to sleep
I'm helpless, I'm helpless, so helpless, sometimes that I weep
Please let me find my own way, my own way to cry
I know we're the dust in the storm, but I think I'll get by.

Verse 3

I can still see the new rose aglow and the dandelion ball in the
grass

Tonight it might leave on the wind but I've got no problem
with that

Tomorrow we'll find a survivor, blow the clock — one o'clock,
two o'clock, three

Pray that my children remember the hours that we spent,
smiling, carefree.

Verse 4

I know that I'm preaching and not really practising that which
I preach

But I'm weary of certainties, knowing tomorrow's not easy to
reach

I saw the great fire in the distance, saw the great lie turn to
dust

If you still think the good book's the answer go back to bed
with that book if you must.

Chorus

'Confirmed'. Me third from right, second row

'Second thoughts'. 'But I think I'll get by' (Photo: Steve Meaney)

Too Old for Fairytales

In 1962 my diary was full. I had pigeons to mind, birds'
eggs to collect, a bow and arrow to make, the makings of
a bonfire to gather. I had the dobber (marbles) season and
the conker season to negotiate and try to end up in the black.
I had to play football, hurling, hoops and tops; go to the
Scouts and the Boys' Confraternity; collect bottles, and sell
them to Mr Merrick in Merrick's Select Bar to make the
money to see Jack Palance in the City Theatre. I had eels and
perch to catch. I had to fit in school and my ecker (homework), raid orchards and enemy camps, and run to Cunneen's
farm twice a day for the milk. No wonder I slept soundly
every night.

There was also something else that I should have been
doing but was desperately trying to avoid, and that was kissing girls. I knew that some day soon I would have to get
round to it. It was being forced upon me. My pals were not
as glued to Audie Murphy or Jeff Chandler as they used to be,
and were leaving the group to go and sit with girls from the
Fairgreen and Garryowen in the back seats of the cinema.

One evening after tea, Mattie O'Brien brought his sister Siobhán along for Joe Cunningham and I to kiss. We adjourned to the part of the Fairgreen field, behind the graveyard, and I drew the short straw to lie in the grass with Siobhán. Joe and Mattie watched from behind the graveyard wall and monitored my progress.

I didn't know where to start. I stretched my arm out, hoping that Siobhán would fall into it, but what worked for John Wayne and Jane Russell didn't work for me. I pushed closer and she drew away. I was far better at cutting eels heads off, or climbing trees, than trying to do this. If Joe and Mattie weren't watching, I would have gladly lied and said that we'd done it, but my reputation was at stake. I had to do something. I jumped on Siobhán, pinned her down and banged our lips together for as long as I could hold my breath. When she finally squirmed out from under me, I said to myself, 'job done,' and raced back to the boys to tell them how dingen it was.

'You done notten.'

'I did. T'was dingen.'

I took up my place with Mattie, while Joe went off to take his turn. It seemed to me that Siobhán didn't squirm quite as much under Joe's attentions. He got started much quicker that I did, and stayed a lot longer. They did a lot more kissing and he came back with his arm over her shoulder. Mattie took his sister back to the Ballysimon Road, and I went home puzzled and troubled.

I had committed a mortal sin and I had nothing to show for it. I also had no intention of telling the priest in Confession. This meant that I was going to commit another if I went to Communion. I'd have to go to Communion sooner and later. I was only thirteen and the flames of Hell were already licking my toes.

I once told a priest in the Augustinian Church on O'Connell Street that I'd had bad thoughts.

'Was there any pollution, my child?'

I didn't know what the word pollution meant, so I chanced a 'no'.

'Well, the next time the devil tempts you with bad thoughts, think of Jesus in the Garden of Gethsemane. Say three Our Fathers for your penance, child.'

'I will, Father.'

Resigning oneself to living in mortal sin for the rest of one's life was a lot for a thirteen-year-old, but I didn't see any way out. It led to a dropping of my moral standards, and the next time I kept company I went straight for the breast. There were new houses being built in O'Connor's field and the unfinished shells were the perfect places for doing all that was forbidden. I took Mary into one of the rooms and put my hand up under her cardigan. I might as well have put it into an electric socket. I couldn't bring myself to think of Jesus in the Garden of Gethsemane, and I knew the mortalers were mounting up. But I was a lost cause anyway, so I kept fondling Mary's underwear until she prised my hand away.

The beautiful electricity that the fondling of Mary's clothed breasts generated set me on the wrong track for a while, and turned my contact with girls into awkward affairs. I wanted to cut to the chase immediately — get fondling, get stiff, and get back to football or fishing. But girls didn't want that. They wanted to talk, kiss a while, talk some more, fondle a small while, and talk. They wanted to tell me about their best friend that they had just fallen out with, and how she was a cheat, and how she was never going to talk to her again in her life, ever. They didn't want to hear about my pigeons, or my Dell Sixty-Four comics, and they had no dobber collection.

If they started crying, I knew it would be ages before I could put my hand up under their cardigans. But it didn't seem to matter. I could never get the hand-under-the-jumper moment right, and many a Juliet stormed off, leaving me in the roof-less shell waiting for my stiffness to die down. I wished I could be like Eddie. He had blond hair and seemed to be always chatting to the girls from the Presentation Convent. Rumour had it that Rosie would put her hand down your pants for a thruppenny bit, and that Eddie had handed over the money.

On Christmas Day 1960, I found a drum and sticks at the bottom of the bed. Santa Claus had got my letter and delivered the goods. It was a beautiful drum, just like the one that I'd seen in Todds' toy department a few weeks before. My mother had taken me shopping for a topcoat and they were getting the toy department ready for Christmas. The drum had a real skin and a lattice of silver, silken rope around its cylinder. The red and blue paint gleamed and it had a musical bump-pah-dee-bump sound. By six o'clock that Christmas Day, I had accidentally put one of the sticks through the skin.

'Jesus, Mary and Joseph,' said my mother.

'He'd break iron,' said my father. 'That's the last time I'll be putting my hand in my pocket for a drum.'

Because it was Christmas Day, I escaped a hiding, but I would have preferred one to making the discovery that I did. When I thought about my father's threat and my visit to Todds, I realised that I'd been hoodwinked, and that the rumours that I'd been hearing about Santy had been true. How did I fall for that coming-down-the-chimney business, when I could see that he was as big as an elephant on the Christmas cards? And the porter and the cake that he scoffed, and getting round the whole world in one night, was all a cod. I should have listened to Decsie. He'd been saying all along that it was your Da who came in through the window. He also had it that girls grew their willies out of their chests when they got older. I'd seen my young sister having her bath in a tub on the kitchen table and there was no sign of any willies coming out of her chest. Decsie was an excitable boy and a mine of misinformation.

The following year I was given a ten-shilling note for my Christmas box. I was told to get whatever I wanted, including the football socks I'd been asking for. I felt doubly cheated. There was no Santy and I was now paying for something that was normally my mother's remit. The next year I was given a pound note, but the things that I really wanted were no longer toys, and cost a lot more than a pound note. I bought a Stanley Gibbons Stamp Collection book and answered ads in *The Hotspur* comic to become a Stamp Approvals Salesman. So strangers wrote to me and sent me fat packages which were addressed to Master Michael Hanley. They put an E in the Hanly, but the packages were for me. I took them to my bedroom and pored over the contents. It wasn't Santy but the correspondence might as well have been coming from the North Pole; my world was small. I bought a shilling's worth and sent off the postal order and waited for the next package. The novelty soon wore off. I began to receive demanding letters. 'Please Return Approvals Forthwith.' The packages had the print of the bedsprings on them, or had fallen down behind the tallboy. When my father had to cough up a ten-shilling note for a lost Approvals book, my collecting came to an abrupt halt.

Breakfast, for all, was a large bowl of porridge, followed by buttered bread and tea. There were dollops of 'What Did

Delaware' and 'How Much Is That Doggy In The Window'. We heard 'The Laughing Policeman' bursting his sides and Bridie Gallagher singing 'The Boys From The County Armagh'. Voices on the radio bade us drink Irel Coffee and buy Donnelly's Sausages.

My life was changed forever the morning that Hank Marvin cut through this dreary musical pea soup. The sound of 'Apache' hit me in the stomach like a heavyweight punch. I went to school drunk. While Mr Horan was taking the class through *An Bun Graiméar, Caibidil 3*, the sound of the Stratocaster kept returning to bewitch me. I heard 'Apache' again that night on Radio Luxembourg and I took another blow to the gut. Every time I heard the sound I was mesmerised. Outside the warm cocoon of those fat notes, my world seemed dreary. I looked at my pigeons — sad and bedraggled in the rain — and suddenly they became dull creatures. My Tristan da Cunha and Nyasaland stamps lost their glow. There was a new electric language; one which I didn't have to speak to, it spoke to me.

My brother Noel had been given a cheap guitar for Christmas, which he quickly abandoned when he discovered that playing it required the work of two hands. I rescued it from behind the sitting-room sofa and tackled 'Apache', the tune of which I now knew by heart. My efforts were a huge disappointment. Even when I could play the notes of the first line without stopping, the sound was nothing like the sound that I was hearing on the radio. I didn't realise that Hank B. Marvin (I knew his second initial by now) was playing a real instrument, using a Binson Echo unit, and feeding the notes through a Vox AC30. He could play as well. On my £2.10 Russian Musik Instrumentavich, it was an uphill battle. I was close to giving up when my namesake Michael Hanly, my father's nephew, took a book from his pocket one night and threw it on the kitchen table.

'One of the lads in work said that this might help you. I was telling them you were going to be the next Elvis.'

The pamphlet was called *Skiff Rock Guitar Tutor For Beginners*. On the cover was a drawing of a man playing a guitar, while two young women looked on approvingly. After an introduction about the endless hours of pleasure that were to be had in getting to know one's instrument and entertaining one's friends, there were two pages on how to tune your instrument. I'd never tuned mine, so it was no wonder I couldn't get it to sound like Hank Marvin's. I tuned it up and learned the chord of D. My mother taught me the tune of the 'Red River Valley' and I was off.

My father coughed up again for my first real instrument.

'Doesn't it keep him off the streets?'

He handed over a ten-shilling note every week to Peter Dempsey, who had a small music store in Mallow Street, Limerick, and Peter ordered my Hagstrom Twelve-String. It cost 63 guineas and was far more beautiful in the flesh than in its black and white catalogue photograph.

I learned the chords of A minor, E minor and my favourite chord of all, B7. 'Apache' sounded better but there were a lot of empty spaces where rhythm guitarist, Bruce Welch, should have been. One night Jimmy Saville announced that he was going to play a disc for all the fab guys and gals out there, by four fab guys from Liverpool. The disc was 'Love Me Do'. I was saved.

Too Old for Fairytales

Verse 1
So easy led, put to bed
And told that Santa Claus is on his way
He knew my name, but only came
To those who still believe I hear my mother say
Sure enough, he did his stuff
That night I heard those sleighbells on the roof
So good so far, one eye closed, one eye ajar
I see my father's shadow leaving, blowing all the proof.

Chorus
Now I'm too old for fairytales
And still too young to dance
I stand in limbo, white shirt and corduroy pants
Now it's cash up front, no more red ribbon to undo
Should have kept my eye closed
For another year or two, for another year or two.

Verse 2
So ill at ease, hard to please
I miss the magic money just can't buy
And Joan next door, a child no more
Is suddenly more beautiful that Rudolf's eye
But what to say, what game to play
My broken china doll has closed up shop
I stand and stare, check the ground for nothing there
She looks at me as if to say, 'When will the penny drop?'

Chorus

Addend

Love, love me do, I had to wait for 'Love Me Do'
Love, love me do, I had to wait for 'Love Me Do'

'White shirt and corduroy pants'. Holiday with my cousins, the O'Reillys, Quilty, Co. Clare

Mineral break, Cruises's Hotel, Limerick

Scouting days. David centre, me behind, Noel to my right

SHELLAKABOOKEE BOY

He was slow to walk so she hauled him on her hip from Chesapeake to the departures area in Kennedy Airport. He was Thomas Edward Westropp-Bennett, aged two, and he was in the loving care of his mother Marie. She sighed deeply when she saw the familiar greens at the Aer Lingus desk, and deeper still as she caught a glimpse of the 747 on the tarmac. When she finally found the seats for her other two children, Mistley aged six, Ashleigh aged four, her sense of relief was overwhelming. On either side of her were the other passengers, who were already sniffing the air with a mixture of disapproval and disdain at having drawn the short straw, being stuck with a row full of children for the next five hours. All Marie could do was try not to catch their eyes for the duration, and pray that Thomas and Ashleigh would not act up. Mistley was old enough to be of help, and she was. Marie and the children had just spent the previous six hours in a car with her husband, Richard, whom she was leaving, and the journey from Chesapeake to Kennedy was fraught and silent for the most part, sometimes interrupted by his pleadings to her to change her mind and give it one last shot. She was not for turning.

Leaving a husband is one thing, but leaving a husband and hauling your three children back to the village of Thomastown, Co. Kilkenny, to become a single mother in the year 1987, was the act of a very brave and single-minded woman. Today, sixteen years later, I can vouch for that fact.

When Marie returned to Thomastown, she was coming back to her hometown. Her situation was not a happy one, but at least she had some familiar touchstones to cling to. There was a plethora of aunts and uncles who were as supportive and as understanding as their old-fashioned mores would allow.

There was her father Mick, and her brothers Tony and John. Despite this, she was essentially on her lonesome, and had to make a home of whatever accommodation could be found. She had to put food in their mouths and set the children up in schools and pre-schools and do whatever ferrying was necessary. Richard was financially supportive, but 3,000 miles removed. Her father Mick would have been of a mind to ask her why she wasn't at her husband's side, 'sure I know things are bad, but wouldn't ye be better off together all the same, isn't that what marriage is all about?' Apart from a few steadfast friends, emotionally, Marie was paddling her own canoe. How in the light of all this she managed to maintain a smile so big and sunny as to knock me off my barstool is one of life's beautiful mysteries, which I'm not about to tamper with . . . but I'm jumping the gun.

The baby, Thomas, didn't sit up until he was a year old. He was a late developer. These days when the beautiful, 6' 1", athletic, thin-as-a-pencil Thomas jokes that he was no trouble as a child, Marie's good-humoured riposte is quick and merciless:

'Thomas, now that you're a fine thing, I can now safely tell you that you were a lump of a child. Muggins here had to drag you round on her back, 'til I was left with no option but to buck you off. I was like a Sherpa going round Thomastown.' This familiar utterance never fails to delight him.

When I sidled, crablike, into Marie's life in 1989, Thomas was nearly five years old. He was a little lardy but he was no longer a lump, though he preferred to shout requests for things rather than come running. The bane of his life at this particular time was his sister Ashleigh. She interfered with whatever games he was playing, hijacked some of his things for her own games, and generally drove him nuts. I heard Thomas before I met him. I was sitting in the front room of Brook House (sounds posh, but it was a damp, over-ventilated, semi-ruin that Marie had somehow made habitable), when I heard a kind of primal scream coming from the top of the stairs.

ASHLEEEEEEEEEEEEEEEEEEEE !!!!!!!!!!!!!!

What took me aback was the fact that this human sound, which I interpreted as a cry of great distress, went unnoticed by the mother of the species, or if she had heard, and there was no way that she could not have, then she was making a very good job of feigning indifference.

ASHLEEEEEEEEEEEEEEEEEEEE!!!!!!!!!!!!!!!

Screaming children unnerve me. Fighting children do the same. Other people's screaming, fighting children make me run. But here I am a-courting and I'm waiting for cues to find out what's normal. Shouting seemed to be the norm in Brook House.

ASHLEEEEEEEEEEEEEEEEEEE!!!!!!!!!!!!!!!!!!!

'What's that?' I venture, with as little surprise as I can manage.

'Oh, that sounds like Thomas.'

'Do you think he's ok?' I tiptoe. What I wanted to say was: 'How can you listen to that all day?' But it was early days yet.

'Oh, he's fine. Ashleigh has probably stood on one of his shellakabookees.'

Well, that explained it. If Ashleigh was standing on one of Thomas's testicles, then the great scream that was shaking the ivy on the walls of Brook House was appropriate. Still, earth mother didn't seem to be too concerned about Thomas's future as a father, so it had to be something else. A shellaka-bookee, however, is not a slang word for testicle, but the real word for a Kilkenny snail. (The spelling is my own.)

In the Limerick of my childhood, snails were known as shallamuddies. In Midleton, Co. Cork, they're known as shelti-horns, and I'm sure that there is any amount of variations for the word snail throughout the land. I never remember being fond of snails myself but I can understand their attraction for children. When you're a child, you're low to the ground, and a snail is as interesting as anything else that moves in that area. Even when you get to your feet, a snail is far more inter-esting than the back of mother's knee or father's behind. Thomas kept his collection in a biscuit tin with a few plucked pissy-beds (dandelions) and some dock leaves. He brought them to his bedroom at night, and harassed them until his light was put out. He was warned, under pain of death, not to remove the biscuit-tin lid. This warning he duly ignored and when Marie went to Thomas's room on foot of a distress call, she often let out a few distress calls of her own.

Murder crossed her mind, as she frantically searched for something to remove the makings of the French delicacy from her heel. Thomas was not throttled, though Marie would have been well within her rights to claim justifiable provocation at her trial for infanticide, had she flung the negligent snail-keeper down the stairs in a rage; instead, his bad dream was taken to his mother's breast, the lid was replaced and the shellakabookee boy was rocked back to sleep. It's on such nurturing that we thrive, and be you healthy lump or sickly gaunt, there is no medicine quite like mother's time and love.

Thomas was very wary of me. I was to become a new presence in his life and his gut instinct told him to keep me at a distance for the moment. His instincts were bang on and over the coming years I had to earn Thomas's respect. I wasn't warm and patient like his mother, or slow and acquiescent like a shellakabookee. I bristled and snapped like a disturbed grizzly and had a sack-full of learned behaviour from my impatient father. Like an invading male lion, I tried to throw my weight around. If I couldn't kill the former alpha male's seed then I could certainly have a go at setting some new ground rules for the pride. Marie, whose antennae were highly sensitive to the male-control factor, instantly sniffed this tactic out. She jumped on it every time it surfaced, and still does today. I have to continually thank her for helping me to recognise it and deal with it. Marie 'mollycoddled' Thomas, as any normal mother would, and despite the virtual non-stop attention that she lavished on me, I was jealous. I wanted to be mollycoddled too, and furthermore I wanted to be the only one that got the mollycoddling. This was my father's instruction to my mother that I was trying to undo, 'Don't be mollycoddlin' him, whatever you do,' when I was allowed to stay home from school sick.

One morning, not long after we had decided to set up home together, I tried to bully Thomas into having a bowl of porridge, which he clearly didn't want but which I had gone to the trouble of making, and he was going to have it. I threatened him with starvation which he dismissed with what Marie called 'Murphy' stubbornness. Already, at the age of six,

Thomas was confident in his mother's love, and knew that she would provide him with a bowl of cereal that was more to his liking than the bowl of gruel which I was now presenting with the advice that it was 'good for him'.

'This grey crap is far better for you than those chocolate-flavoured balls your mother is going to give you, Thomas!'

It's hard to believe that I was stupid enough to use the argument that 'porridge is good for you' on a six-year-old child, but jealousy is a very negative emotion and the well-spring of the craziest notions.

On another morning, I tried to bully him onto the school bus. Thomas was not of a mind to go to school that morning. It was cold, semi-dark and he wasn't in good form. He reminded me a lot of myself when I was of the same mind as a child. His mother for once was not the one holding his hand and kissing him goodbye, so he decided to dig in his little heels. Despite the efforts of his sisters to persuade him up the steps, Thomas was determined to go back home and have a piece of that warm body, which I was about to have all to myself for the rest of the morning. We returned to the house, stubborn Thomas and his petulant minder.

'What's wrong?'

'His nibs here wouldn't get on the bus,' I announced with a semi-triumphant air.

The subtext of which was, 'Look at what your little bundle of joy has gone and done to you. Because he won't listen to his elders, he's gone and deprived you of my undivided attention for the rest of the morning.' I got the answer that I did not want to hear.

'Give him over here to me, I'll drop him in later.'

An hour later, Marie dropped a relaxed and reassured Thomas into the Kilkenny School Project, where he pottered happily for the rest of the day. One child had been taken care of, while the other child was left to fume quietly with paper and crossword, until his injured manhood could be massaged.

Had Marie been a weaker person in those early years of our relationship, I might have been able to impose a certain joyless regime on our lives, which, in my blindness, would have confirmed my so-called male role, but happily she was strong enough to resist the bullying and with gentle persuasion managed to steer me in a different and more rewarding direction.

Today, with the benefit of hindsight, and no small amount of love and patience, I can see the folly of the imposition of hard and fast rules on children. I also know that children love nothing more than sure boundaries on their behaviour, and the child who is not given this kind of tough love is a lost and troublesome child, and invariably, a disturbed adult. I also think that the education system, especially for the non-academic, is glaringly inept, particularly so in second level. The assessment of all our children by the same yardstick is absurd.

Thomas was lucky enough to spend his primary years at the Kilkenny School Project. I believe that the child-centredness of the multi-denominational ethos, which prevails there, has stood to Thomas and his peers, and is still a help to him as he negotiates his way through adulthood in the American military. Thomas is now a Marine, has been for the last two years. If he can avoid seeing the horrors of action, I believe that Thomas will leave the Marines a strong and rounded individual, with a positive sense of himself and his achievements. When he calls home these days, I find myself talking to an articulate, energised young man; not the mumbling, callow youth that I drove to Shannon Airport. He's been to hell and back in the last couple of years and he's still laughing. But let me sketch in a few more details before we get to Parris Island.

Thomas is not academic. For him the last two years of
school were torture. He had been sidelined by the system and
both Thomas and the system had given up on each other. It
was painful to watch. He did his best to pretend that he was
trying to absorb the meaningless litanies that would have
gotten him enough points to scrape a pass, but he was swimming in wet concrete. He was as aware as we were that
whatever his *métier* was, this was not it, and the sooner that it
was over the better. It was hard to badger him into doing
homework that he neither liked nor understood, and despite
our knowing that Thomas was unbadgerable, we did try to
convince him, from time to time, that this piece of paper, *An
Ardteist*, was an important document that was vital for his
future. He wasn't convinced. My own persuasive powers (we
got on well at this stage) fell on deaf ears since I was in the
same camp as him to begin with.

As soon as the ritual burning of the school uniform was
done, he started 'hangin'. Short of climbing into his pocket
every time that he went to town, we kept as watchful an eye
as possible on him, but we couldn't stop him bringing his bag
full of beer up the river and getting pissed with his mates. He
had as many crashes as journeys on his Katana motorbike, and
the night that the Guards arrived to the front door to tell us
that he had ploughed into a parked car and left the scene of
the accident, I knew we had a normal, healthy, and for the
moment, lucky teenager on our hands. On another occasion,
blinded by the lights of an oncoming truck in Bennettsbridge,
he missed a bend and ricocheted off a concrete wall into the
middle of the road in the fading light. This time he wasn't so
lucky. He lay there momentarily until his mate, following on
behind on another Katana, ploughed his bike into Thomas's
prostrate bones. We sat by his trolley-side in a corridor of St

Luke's Hospital, Marie holding his hand. One more grey hair sprung, one more mothering scar on her heart. You feel relieved when you've managed to steer your children to manhood/ womanhood undamaged, unburned, unmolested, unaddicted but sooner or later there's a sharp reminder that the next ten years are as big a lottery as the preceding ten, and you sigh at the predictability of the lessons that seemingly must be learned the hard way.

A few weeks after finishing his Leaving Cert, Thomas leaves for his annual visit to Richard's home in Chesapeake, Maryland. I drive him to Shannon. I'm going to take the opportunity to have a stepfather-to-stepson chat with him about how, despite the fact that his behaviour has been getting on our nerves, we still think that he's a great guy, 'and, Thomas, you know I did all those . . . you're not the only . . . I remember when I was your age . . .'

Before we reach Callan, about fifteen miles from Thomastown, Thomas has fallen asleep, and doesn't wake up until we reach the 'Get in Lane' sign for Shannon Airport, just outside Bunratty. We have a second breakfast at the air-port café, where he tries to insist on paying for both of us. I abandon all the stepfather-to-stepson stuff and settle for recalling some of Manchester United goalkeeper, Fabien Bartez' most famous errors and Homer Simpson moments for a laugh. We call Marie on the mobile. He listens to her repeated pleas to take care, her repeated expressions of love and her final goodbyes. He hands the phone to me and slips away to cry. I reassure his tearful mother that he's fine. She's as distraught as she was three hours ago when we left the house. This summer's departure has a finality about it that previous summers did not. School is finished for good, he has a razor in his baggage for the little blonde moustache that becomes noticeable about once a month, and he can now lift his mother off the ground. He's about to walk through passport control, the final door. We throw our arms around each other. I'm acutely aware that my own father never did this to me and I'm glad to be able to break that particular cycle. We're both teary. He looks at me and says, 'It's very hard.' I say 'I know.' We both stand for a moment looking at each other, wordless. 'Take care,' I say, echoing his mother's words. He's gone.

The news from Chesapeake is not great. Thomas is bagging burgers in Supermac's. On his days off, he's isolated in Richard's house on the Dupont farm. (Richard is stud manager on the farm and his house is miles from any sort of action that might interest a seventeen-year-old.) There's no lovingly-cooked meat and veg and tasty glass of milk. There are no Tayto crisps in a basket, because there is no basket. There is no fresh-smelling, newly-ironed tee shirt. It's bachelor-pad basics and not a can of beer in sight. He rows with Richard. In Chesapeake there is an open day for the US Marines. His isolation is getting him down. He talks to the recruiting officer in Chesapeake. The officer is an expert in head games and Thomas is like putty in his hands. Thomas flings his last bagged burger at his acned superior in Supermac's and tells him where to shove it. He goes to pump iron and run with his new-found friend, Sergeant Brendlinger. He calls to tell us that enlisting in the US Marines is a possibility. His new-found motivation comes sparking from the mouthpiece. We look at each other trying to mask our deepest fears. We seek the positives. Structure in his life. Get-out-of-bed motivation. A qualification at the end of his stint. A light at the end of what can become the dark tunnel for a seventeen-year-old.

Were Thomas to enlist, I had serious reservations about his ability to handle the forthcoming ordeal. I saw the film *Full Metal Jacket* and found it deeply disturbing. When I heard that he would be going to Parris Island, I immediately had visions of him being bullied, duped, raped and preyed upon. I didn't give him credit for having the inner steel that it would take to get him through the coming three months intact. I'd forgotten that he'd stood up to me at the age of five and told me what to do with my porridge! I'd also forgotten that he'd come through the arduous vetting process for the Mount Juliet caddies and survived intact. Thomas is no pushover, and in the end I was made to eat my private thoughts about him.

He finally put his name to a piece of paper which ties him to the Marines for four years, and disappeared from our radar to one of the toughest drilling outposts in America, Parris Island.

We hold our collective breaths for the next four months as we await the inevitable call from Sergeant Brendlinger: 'Your son has been dismissed for a violation of article 197846 D (xv) of the US Marines Code of Conduct. He used three sheets of Army-Issue toilet paper as opposed to the permitted one and a half, Mam.'

'Your son has been found sleeping on guard duty which is in breach of article 489678 B (vii), Mam.'

'We're sorry, Mam.'

The call never comes. Thomas doesn't fuck up. The postman drops an army-issue envelope through our box. Inside is a page of army-issue writing paper stained with the tears of a seventeen-year-old, homesick child. Marie dries her own and sits down to write today's letter. It's much the same as yesterday's. Every dog scratch is mentioned. The latest egg-count from the breeding budgies. Colds, cuts, falls, recoveries.

Progress reports on the humdrum until three pages are full. Ellen and Katie draw animal pictures for him and the fat comforting package is sent. Every couple of weeks I invent some unlikely scenarios of Thomastown life, which I hope will give him a laugh. I recount the latest Bartez error, and tell him that Thomastown Celtic have turned down an offer from Alex for their wonderful goalkeeper, but that they might consider letting him go if there's a cash offer, with Sebastian Veron and Nicky Butt thrown in. Thomastown Celtic know the value of a safe pair of hands! I make them as daft and outrageous as I can, and the feedback is positive.

His own accounts of life are grim. Endless drilling and humiliation. Five-mile humps with gear, and more humiliation. Fat guys fucking up. Fat guys stealing doughnuts while on fat-guy rations. Fat guys trying to ease the aching in their crying bellies and getting caught, landing the platoon in a shitload of trouble and two extra hours of drill. Fat guys are bad, fucking news. Sand flies, punishment and more humiliation. Snippets of praise are as rare as a benign sandfly. Homesickness, tears, more homesickness.

At last, a five-minute phone call.

'I'm strongly motivated, Mum, and I'm gonna make you proud.'

'Thomas, I want to tell you that I was proud of you the moment that you were born. I've been proud of you every day of your life since. I love you and I will always be proud of you.'

'I thought you said that I was lump?' he asks, playfully.

'Of course you were a lump, but you were a beautiful lump, and you were my lump and if you were forever a lump, I'd love you still.'

He's not really listening. I'm eavesdropping on the other phone. He wants to do the talking. He wants to tell his mother about how proud she is going to be. She listens. She'd give an eye tooth to hold him. She knows her strengths. Her boundless ability to give, to comfort, to listen, to reassure. It's her *métier*. Motherhood. Her element.

'And we're thinking of you too, Thomas, and we love you. Yes, yes, we love you too.'

On Friday, 22 February 2001, at 15.20 hours American time, our beloved Thomas became Private Thomas Westropp-Bennett and joined his 63 fellow graduates for a ceremonial march past on the sprawling drill area of Parris Island. Marie, Ellen and Katie flew to America for his graduation, and Richard came down from Chesapeake with Allan, one of Thomas's pre-Parris Island mentors. We didn't tell Thomas that Ellen and Katie were going to be there. He broke ranks when he saw them, probably violating another article of the US Marine code by giving the little sisters that he loves the squeeze of their life. However, he wasn't thrown in the clinker for it. It's joy all round. Everyone loves a winner and everyone is proud of 'Westropp' as he has become affectionately known. He's been to hell and back and come out the other end. We'd be naive to think that he's the same; he's not. He's older, tougher, wiser and stronger than his years. He's mixing it with the men, and, at eighteen years, is being asked to lead some of them. To his mother, he is still her Shellakabookee Boy.

She watches him march past along with his fellow Marines of 1014 B Bravo Company. She has no trouble picking him out: he is straight as a die and proud that his mother is a witness. Her eyes fill as she tries to focus her camera.

On Tuesday, 11 September 2001, at 8.46 a.m., Al Qaeda do their worst.

Shellakabookee Boy

Verse 1

He was slow to walk so she hauled him on her hip
He was heavy then but she never let him slip
It's no wonder it's so hard for her to loosen her grip
On her shellakabookee boy
Every garden snail he laid out on a plate
'Don't be shy,' he said, 'I can wait, I can wait.'
Then one day all by himself he stood and opened the gate
Her shellakabookee boy
Then she coaxed him towards the school
Found his mittens, found his coat
Urged him towards the pool.
Saw him flounder, helped him float
When at last he walked on water
She went, My, Oh My, Oh My.

Chorus

Every mother has a boy in the field, in the field
And all she has to hold is a picture of his charms
Every boy has a mother back at home, back at home
And all he wants to do is lie there in her arms
All he wants to do is lie there in her arms.

Verse 2

Parris Island's not the place for gentle hearts
Tender mercies, trampled on, torn apart
Every homesick tear that's shed's another stain on the chart
Of a shellakabookee boy
They take everything, all your clothes, all your hair
Your dignity, every mask you've learned to wear

'Til you're naked on parade and there's no more that they can
    tear
From a shellakabookee boy
They dress you down, fuck you over
'Til you're sparking like a fuse
Reassemble, reassure you, march you out in your dress blues
In his arms on graduation
She goes, My, Oh My, Oh My.

Addend
But she's no say in the matter any more
And a million mothers' kisses never stopped
The unforgiving ricochets of war
And when the good news or the bad comes to her door
She goes, My, Oh My, Oh My.

'He was slow to walk'

'Love you too, buddy.'
Thomas's first visit
home from Parris
Island

Graduation Day. Ellen, Tom and Katie

Private Westropp-Bennett, Thomas

TRYING TO GET TO ST NAZAIRE

In 1973 I travelled to France for the first time. I went with guitarist/singer Mícheál Ó Domhnaill and Cathal Goan. Mícheál and myself were the members of a duo called Monroe, and we'd recorded an album with Polydor, which was yet to be released and which would be called *Celtic Folkweave*. We were at a loose end and were mad to travel, so Mícheál's sister Tríona suggested that we go to Brittany while we awaited the album's release. She had a boyfriend at the time called Serge Cariou, who lived in the tiny village of Dirinon, ten kilometres from Brest, and it was to Serge's gate lodge that we repaired for the summer months. Cathal played the tin whistle and came along for the ride. About a month into our sojourn, piper Paddy Keenan arrived with his Ballyfermot friend, singer Liam Weldon. Cathal was immediately given his P45 and Paddy was installed as a member of Monroe. Cathal's summary dismissal didn't cause any friction as he was, as he'd say himself, a 'kiss-me-arse of a whistle player' and was only kicking his heels while he awaited his Celtic Studies results from UCD; he had his eye on other things, including Mícheál's sister, Máighréad.

Paddy, however, was the real deal. He played with his father John, and his brothers, Johnny and Thomas. They were known as 'The Pavees' and they played in Slattery's Pub, in Capel Street, and other musical venues in Dublin. They were first-generation settled travellers and Paddy was justifiably proud of the piping tradition from which he came. Serge was diligent enough and before long Monroe was playing at every shindig and Fest-Noz in Brittany. He ferried us from gig to gig in his powerful Citroen, and kept the hedges of Brittany well trimmed.

For me the Brittany experience was hugely liberating. The stifling shackles of life at home, whether real or imagined, were flung like rags into the Dirinon trees as I began to realise that the world was my oyster. I was far too young to appreciate the beauty of what France had to offer, but I threw myself into the wine, women and song part of it with a will, deciding to hold paintings, historical buildings and haute cuisine for another time. Every young French girl who tried to speak English to me made me go weak at the knees, but somehow I seemed to have the courage to hold their eyes for that extra telling moment longer than I did at home. I helped them finish the sentences which they found most difficult and guided them through the thorny copses of the English language, with the patience of a butterfly catcher. Realising how attractive their stumbling efforts in English were to me, it wasn't too long before I started to struggle with a few French sentences myself in the hope that it worked both ways. I had done a couple of years of French at school, but had paid it little heed.

'*Je m'appelle Mick*' was as good a starting point as any, and when they responded with 'how you pronounce . . . *ah, Meeek,*' I was a gonner.

Serge explained menus, ordered drinks, negotiated fees and generally dogsbodied, so we didn't have to become involved in the everyday if we didn't want to, but since I couldn't dance, I was anxious to impress in other ways.

I did have other problems to negotiate as well. For a musician, I'm a very early riser. No matter how much Ricard or Kronenbourg I put away, I was invariably awake by sun-up, and found myself slaking my thirst with the early morning dew, in the little country lanes around Dirinon, on many an occasion. I met startled locals beginning their daily farming chores, beret-topped, in fresh Mao-type suits, and the unlit remains of a yellow Gitane glued to their bottom lip. I usually greeted them with a nod of the head and a 'Hello', whereupon they started checking for my white-coated minders and increased their pedal work-rate.

As soon as the local grocery store opened its doors, I was in like a thirsty Irishman on Good Friday. I wasn't after drink but the full Irish breakfast. The store looked as though it had been airlifted from Knockcrockery to Dirinon. It was a bar, haberdashery, grocery, post office and, no doubt, had a spare coffin or two out back. The lady of the store had 'null' English and our exchanges were initially amusing, latterly tetchy. I couldn't find a proper sausage or a rasher with some meat on it. On my first couple of visits she allowed me inside the counter to inspect what she had after much puzzlement — that privilege was quickly withdrawn when I didn't make a purchase. I didn't have the language to thank her properly for her indulgence and my 'I'll see you tomorrow' didn't cut any of the ice, which was now starting to form between us.

Cookeen was another thing that I couldn't find and it didn't have a French equivalent, since there is no such thing as a 'Breton Fry'. And also, cooking in oil is a relatively new phenomenon in Ireland. When I left home, my mother was still melting two half-pound slabs of Cookeen to do the Friday chips. There was a basket of varicoloured eggs on the counter, with genuine chickenshit and feathers, which gave me false hope. I had real tea, which my mother sent me from home, real eggs, real tomatoes, I was only a pudding ring short of the real deal, but I felt deprived.

I banged my Irish head off a French stone wall for a couple of months. I cooked the eggs in a 'stick' frying pan (the opposite to non-stick), with butter as a dripping substitute, until the contents of the pan — eggs, so-called rashers and tomatoes — became an immovable red and yellow mess. The meatless rashers shrivelled into bacon fries. The tomatoes burned on one side and didn't thaw on the other. The egg yokes broke and spread, and I was more often tempted to frame the result rather than eat it. There was one plus; the sight of the finished article sent Mícheál and Cathal dashing for the front door, so I had the entire contents to myself. Despite all these setbacks I continued to haunt the grocery-store Madame until she dreaded the sight of me and began to dismiss me with some French phrases that would later come in useful in whatever bar brawl I'd gotten myself into.

Then one day I had a Damascus-like conversion. I had not been enjoying my John Players cigarettes for a while; they didn't seem to combine very well with Ricard, and they were far more expensive than the native brands. Players, pints and a feed of bacon and cabbage mix; Ricard, sandwich jambon, and Gauloise mix; both combinations give you heartburn that you recognise. So I told my mother to stop sending me

Halpins Gold Blend, and I bought a packet of Blue Gauloise. I went to the local and *toute une claque j'ai commencé à parler une 'tit peut français.*

Unfortunately, by now it was time to go home. The festival season was winding down and the winter was setting in, but whatever happened, I vowed to return.

Monroe returned to Ireland to a gigless winter. *Celtic Folkweave* was released in our absence to the sound of one hand clapping. Without work, Mícheál and I drifted apart, but some of the tracks from the album had their day in the sun. Our take on a set of Breton dances became the signature tune for a popular traditional programme called *The Long Note*. Our version of a piece of Scottish mouth music, 'Am Bothan A B'aig Fionnaghuala', was unusual enough to turn some of the more sceptical heads. The Bothy Band was later to do a speedier version which became a showstopper. But musically, I was now at sea. Mícheál had been a crutch in an area that I knew nothing about. I had taken another step in an effort to find a voice of my own, but confusion reigned. I'd been to Liverpool, Route 66 and the Dust Bowl. I'd been singing about Fire and Rain, and looking for America, and I was now Roving out on May mornings and thinking about Kissing in the Morning Early. I'd been round the world for sport. There was plenty of sport but very little musical progress. All around me were young-sters, fired by the fact that Planxty had made the playing of traditional music hip, tootling flutes and wrestling with con-certinas and sets of pipes like never before. There was also no shortage of Donal Lunny and Mícheál Ó Domhnaill clones doing their best to trip them up, but the fluters and the fiddlers usually closed their eyes and carried on regardless.

I had no place in this milieu. My voice had no presence and couldn't be heard over a clothes-line. When a real singer, such

as Diarmuid Ó Súilleabháin, hushed the madding crowd with
a ten-verse epic in a language that 90 per cent of the natives
didn't understand, I knew I had a long way to go. As soon as
the cold winds of February were over, I took the easy option
and returned to Brittany.

Mick Hanly meant nothing to the Bretons who'd seen
Monroe the previous summer; even *Meeek* Hanly couldn't
charm anyone into giving him some musical work.
Furthermore, March was not a good time, so when Maryvonne
Salaun drove me to the town of Douarnenez, which is a fishing port about 20 kilometres from Quimper, I was glad to
pick up some work unloading the nightly boats, *pour gagner
des sous*. I stayed in Douarnenez, on and off, for the next
two years and my stay there was to prove as happy an experience as I've ever had in my life. I grew to love Douarnenez,
and a bunch of people in it who welcomed me into their
company with an openness and affection that was more
Irish than French. I learned French, became French, played
darts in French, slept with girls in broken French, while they
slept with me in broken English. I went to work on the port
as part of *'la deuxième équipe'*. It was casual night-work. It was
also cold, dreary and dangerous work for a guitar player.
There was no shortage of gravel-voiced workmates who were
a couple of fingers short of the full deck, and I didn't really
want to know how they'd disposed of the missing ones so
I didn't ask, but I wasn't blind. Large, heavy, iron baskets
suspended on quayside derricks were juggled from hold to
quayside at speed; the catch, which kept the basket upright,
was released and the contents dumped into square containers.
It was carelessness around this particular nasty piece of
equipment that turned guitar-playing digits to fish fingers in
the blink of an eye.

The apprenticeship for this particular task was a ten-minute introductory course, conducted in French. The natives, though not hostile, were not prepared to make allowances for a stranger with poor French, and if I didn't understand whatever command or warning that I was given, then the two-ton basket might miss me by a couple of centimetres, or a load of fish would fall at my feet and not in the basket that it was supposed to land in. Having to pick them up did not mean that *Mo Dhuine* (*Mo Dhuine* is the Irish for 'my person' — the polite English equivalent is 'yer man') stopped dipping in the hold for a new load; you picked up what you could between deliveries and hoped you got the quayside cleared before the foreman came by. I met these near-accidents with a look of contempt to the perpetrator. It was usually returned with interest and a Gallic shrug, which immediately went into my vocabulary of French body movements. When I can't remember or don't know the appropriate French word, I shrug and leave the French to put a meaning on it.

Sometimes we did the bigger tunnyboats, and they were bone-chilling. On the tunnyboats you worked one hour on, one hour off. You were given the hour off to thaw out. Those who had homes sped away on their mopeds for 50 minutes by the fire; those who were homeless repaired to one of the quay-side bars to thaw out with the help of alcohol. Since the last open bar shut at two o'clock, you had to stock up for the last three hours during your last hour off. From two o'clock to five you had to keep your wits about you. Nearly everyone was over the limit, but their tasks were so specific that they could do them in their sleep: that's when they lost the fingers. There were lots of close shaves and lots of shouting, but I never saw an accident. By the time summer arrived, I thought that I'd have a bag full of Breton sea shanties, but I never heard anyone singing on the job; whistling monotonously yes, but no singing.

It was a dour stint, but my French improved rapidly and the pay, which was excellent, kept the wolf from Erwan's door. Erwan Kervalla was my minder and mentor around this time. He and his partner, Michelle Charles Do, gave me a room in the house that they were renting. Erwan roadied for Alan Stivell and had hours similar to mine. We went back and forth to Bar de la Rade and played darts in the basement of the house. Before long I was able to count and add in French better than himself. I had an eye-opener of a French lesson one day in a tobacco shop. I rehearsed a French sentence in order to make my purchase and pushed open the glass door with a certain amount of confidence.

'*Je veux acheter un paquet Gauloise, s'il vous plaît.*'

'*Du blond ou du bleu?*' she retorted. I was '*mot*'less.

'Oh, forget it. I'll be back tomorrow.' I left the shop effing and blinding, frustrated at my lack of progress. I related my tale of woe to Erwan when I got home.

'*Bah, qu'est-ce que tu cherche, toi? Va être un prof, ou fumer?* (*Bah*, what are you looking to be? A professor or do you want a smoke?)

'*Il faut dire du Gauloise, seulement, mon vieux.*' (Just say Gauloise, my friend.)

I returned the following day and put Erwan's advice to work.

'*Du Gauloise,*' I said, with a shrug.

In a flash, a brand new packet of blue Gauloise was thrown on the counter.

'*Un franc quarant, monsieur, s'il vous plaît.*'

Alors! This was a strange discovery because French language etiquette is far more rigorous than our own. They use *vous* when addressing strangers and *tu* when addressing those whom they know well. I suppose our equivalent is calling somebody Mr or Mrs instead of his or her proper Christian name. I never got used to the *tu* and *vous* and to this day I trample all over the convention with my familiarity. I've never met anyone who pulled me up on it, but maybe that's because they're too mannerly, or maybe it's because the Bretons are friendlier than the rest of the French.

Also, I've never lived in any other region of France for long enough to check it out.

Overall, I'd say that I fared much better at making myself understood when I used less French and more gestures and meaningless noises (noises that are not in the dictionary), than when I used unanimated French. In fact it is possible to get by with no French at all. The appropriate *Bah*, accompanied by the appropriate movement of the shoulders followed by a long enough silence will usually give your listener the impression that you know what's going on. If this *pièce du théâtre* is met with another *pièce du théâtre*, which is the real thing, then throw in an *Oh* followed by a *Bah*, and see how you get on. You might be given a packet of Gauloise instead of a pound of tomatoes but you'll feel better. *Bah* and *Oh* are the two most important words you will ever learn in French. Memorise them and practise the rest in front of the mirror.

My local was a bar on the port called La Rade. It was really a hotel, which was owned and run by Micheline and Robert Hascoet. La Rade is also known as Chez Micheline, and at the time of my sojourn was the hangout for a lot of the local music-loving, hippy types. Robert did the cooking and Micheline ran the bar. She was a kind of mother-away-from-home for all of us. She ran a tight ship and was forever scolding those who drank too much or acted the maggot, for whatever reason. She was also kind and caring to those who were in need of comforting, and not having money for the moment didn't prevent one having a drink there. Her greeting to me was always:

'*Tu as soif, mignon?* (Are you thirsty, pet?)'

'*J'ai pas du sous, Miche.* (I'm broke, Miche.)'

'*Oui, mais tu prends quelque chose, comme même?* (But you'll have something, just the same.)'

(Recently, I went to Douarnenez for Micheline's 78th birthday. Her daughter Marisse organised a gathering of all the musicians who used to frequent La Rade in the 70s. It was a superb couple of days, and it seemed as though we'd all just stepped out for a few moments, and returned having had a severe haircut. And that was only the women.)

La Rade was my office, and Micheline was my unofficial agent; the only problem was that I didn't understand Micheline's French very well. I did a lot of *Bah*ing and *Oh*ing and often ended up with half a baguette instead of the whole enchilada; found myself a day too early; four hours too late, or in the wrong Ploughinon. It always took a sizeable amount of Ricard to sort out the misunderstandings and I comforted myself with the thought that my French was improving all the time.

It was Micheline who took the call from the organisers of a music festival in St Nazaire. It was lucrative enough to make the long haul, and because the gig was on a Sunday, I decided to take the train, or as it turned out, several trains. I normally hitched to gigs, at my leisure, arriving a day early, leaving the day after, or not leaving for a week, depending on the post-gig fallout.

For the non-native, Sundays in France are strange affairs. It's a family day. It's a prolonged eating day. It's a 'talking among themselves about what they're about to eat, what they're eating, and what they've just eaten' day. If you are not a family member, and not well versed in the gastronomical nuances of *une certaine sauce* or a *Coquille Saint-Jacques*, then Sunday invitations to dinner should be avoided. Even in restaurants, the lone Sunday diner attracts as much attention as an arsonist, or some such deviant, on his day off. Of course all this talking and eating means that there's nobody on the move, so naturally, hitching is a nightmare. I often spent hours outside some small village called 'Something-Sur-This or That' listening to the larks, and nodding to passing farmers who all had the look of 'I'm normally not out on my bike on Sundays, but my wife forgot *une certaine chose pour la sauce* and I'm on my way to get Mrs Chouchen to open the shop.'

On this particular Sunday, the Quimper ticket seller was the perfect manifestation of my worst fears. Did you ever hand over your money to a ticket seller, who suddenly excuses himself, shuts the hatch for security reasons, then emerges by a door next to the hatch and strolls off into the bowels of the railway concourse with the air of a man who's finally cracked, and decided to hand in his notice? You didn't? Well, go to Quimper station and ask for a ticket to St Nazaire. I can promise you that the ticket seller will say *'Excusez moi'* and disappear out of your life forever.

I don't travel by rail anymore. Some people love trains. I love reading about people travelling in trains; I love the sound of trains; I take solace in the comings and going of the Thomastown train, but these days I give travelling by train a miss. Apart from the friendly ticket sellers, I always feel trapped in a railway carriage. Once you choose your seat on a train, that's it. Whoever decides thereafter to slide in beside you, or sit opposite you, is inevitably your companion for

the next couple of hours, and I seem to attract defiant law-
breaking smokers, children with Attention Deficit Disorder,
transistor-toting skinheads, and mobile carrying nerds — all
at the same time.

There have been a few occasions when I've been too drunk to
perform. I'm not proud of the fact and I didn't make a habit
of it. There have been many occasions when I've been drunk
by the end of a performance, and that was all to do with
thinking that performing and drinking were intrinsically
linked and that one helped the other; the real trick was getting the balance right. I gave up drinking before gigs about
fifteen years ago, but if there is anybody out there who feels
like correcting that statement, be my guest; my memory isn't
all that great. I was approaching my 40s and my eyesight had
suddenly deteriorated. I remember breaking a string towards
the end of a gig one night in The Béal Bocht in Dublin, and
being unable to find the hole in the machine-head of the
guitar to thread the new string through. (Today I can't find
the machine head and that's nothing to do with drink.) I'd
gotten the balance perfect: the perfect balance of drunkenness
and blindness, and it took me so long to repair the damage
that I lost whatever head of steam I'd built up, and blew the
gig. So I stopped drinking before gigs and started to speed-
drink post-gig instead.

I could blame the St Nazaire disaster on one missed train,
but that would be simplifying things. The real damage was
done with a bottle of Jaegermeister on my way from Quimper
to Lorient. I never liked Jaegermeister, but somebody once
told me that it was nutritional, and that it gave one a lift, so
now and again I'd pick up the odd bottle in the supermarket
in case of a dip. I could also describe the rest of the day to

you but I hope the song does that. One thing that did stick in my mind about the journey was that when I boarded the train in Quimper there were a half-dozen natives in my compartment, who'd postponed Sunday dinner. By the time the train reached Lorient, I'd half-finished the bottle of Jaegermeister and all the passengers had disembarked. I had the compartment to myself, which I have to say is how I like it. However, as I made my way through the train in search of further refreshments, I began to realise that I'd seen some of the passengers before, and they had Jaegermeister-fright written all over them. My journey to St Nazaire is now in the file, labelled 'very hazy'.

I have to come clean before I close and say that I have no idea what the name of the town was where I missed my connection. I looked up the map and found St Nicolas-de-Redon, and I thought it sang well. Catherine's real name was probably Ingrid, but we won't let these petty details get in the way of the story.

Trying to Get to St Nazaire

Verse 1

I ask myself why is that carriage leaving at exactly the same time as my next connection's due

I'm on the wrong side of the tracks and it's too much of a coincidence 'cause it's leaving right on cue

I know the consequences if I've blown one more arrival, there won't be a welcoming party there

I'm in St Nicolas-de-Redon, and I'm trying to get to St Nazaire.

Verse 2

I make some enquiries in the best French that I can muster, *mais elle dit 'je ne comprends pas'*

I guess she smells the alcohol, thinks I'm English, shuts the hatch, *c'est le dimanche, et bah*

She disappears but I think I understand enough to catch the phrase *Je reviens toute à l'heure*

In St Nicolas-de-Redon, trying to get to St Nazaire.

Verse 3

Have you ever spent a Sunday afternoon in France, in a station, that's barely made it onto the map

Well I can tell you that you'll have time to write the novel, write the second and the third, and do your first redraft

The natives vanish into the ether with their grannies and their children for an afternoon's *fruits de mer*

In St Nicolas-de-Redon, trying to get to St Nazaire.

Verse 4

I'm two hours into a four-hour wait, half my stash is gone,
   there's a crackling on the gravel and a saint appears
She reads the *'fermé'* sign, turns around to look at me, with a
   smile that says 'I'm not as wet as you around the ears'
She's Catherine from Scandinavia and she's on her way to see
   an Irish guy in concert,
Elle dit, 'C'est en plein air'
I tell her I'm her man and I'm trying to get to St Nazaire.

Verse 5

It's rarely that I get drunk enough to miss the boat, or as in
   this case miss the second train, but I'm about to do just
   that
I've sunken into the eyes of Catherine, her broken English,
   and everything beneath her brown felt hat
I ask her to be my manager, be my mistress, tell her not to
   worry, swear hand on heart that I'll get her there
In St Nicolas-de-Redon, trying to get to St Nazaire.

Verse 6

There's a moment when you realise that something you
   thought was once within your grasp has suddenly passed
   you by
And in alcohol it's compounded by the fact that you're
   reduced to working with the aid of just one good eye
I take my guitar from my case; try to break a leg or two, while
   the natives look elsewhere
In St Nicolas-de-Redon, trying to get to St Nazaire.

Verse 7

She gets me to the gig somehow, what a manager, what a
    stroke, but I'm not the only one that's having one
'*Il sont fous les Irlandais, qu'est-ce qu'on fait?*' There's consterna-
    tion so they put me in a caravan
When I wake up I realise that my body has arrived intact but
    my mind is still way back there
In St Nicolas-de-Redon, trying to get to St Nazaire.

Verse 8

I'll spare you the rest of the gory details, but t'was Catherine
    who took the bullets, I got out alive
We had a relationship of sorts, we shared sardines from a can,
    some *chocolat-pain-beurre*, but it failed to thrive
Today, I check the map just to see how many miles it is from
    a semblance of hope to blank despair
It could be forty, maybe less
From St Nicolas-de-Redon,
But it might as well be a million when you're in your cups
And you're trying to get to St Nazaire.

Monroe cycling to France!

'Hairy Times' Planxty, with driver Johnny Divilly, and support act. Savoy Cinema, Limerick, 9 February 1973

Haute cuisine avec chapeau Irlandais

I Am, I Am

A few years ago I said something at the table at home in Station Road which stopped my wife in her tracks and, momentarily, caused the rest of the assembled to pause in their papadam-crunching:

'Do you know when you're driving alone? Do you ever get the feeling that your hands might lose the run of themselves and pull the steering wheel into the path of the next oncoming truck?'

'You mean suicide?'

'No, I don't mean suicide. This is not premeditated. It's similar to the feeling that I get when I go too close to the edge of a cliff; a feeling that something is going to hijack the controls and make me jump.'

'You do mean suicide?'

'No, no. I'm talking about something different, and it's not a suicidal urge.'

'Hmmmm.'

As the crunching recommenced, only my brother David acknowledged experiencing something similar. No debate ensued but 'I Am, I Am' was written shortly afterwards.

'Let's go to Browne's Diner and have a beer,' said Jim Rooney, on our way in from Nashville Airport.

'I'm on the dry,' I said.

'They got food too,' Jim said, dryly.

Back then, being on the dry was one of those dreadful endurance tests that I had to take on every few years in order to reassure myself that I was in control. It was usually triggered by a bout of alcohol poisoning, and the subsequent feeling was so bad that going without was easy to begin with. After a few weeks, I'd be feeling well enough to say 'never again'. My resolve was unshakeable. After a few months, my rude good health, and sense of wellbeing, was such that it called for a celebration.

Jim Rooney, or Rooney to his many, many friends, was the only contact I had when I went to Nashville for the first time in 1991. Guitarist Philip Donnelly, who had spent years in Nashville as a much sought-after session player, had given me Jim's number.

'If you're looking for anybody in Nashville, Rooney will probably know him, and more importantly, will know whether or not you should be looking for him.'

I rang Jim from Boston, where I was doing a couple of concerts.

'Come right on down.'

I had met Jim very briefly some years before. He was on the road with banjo player Bill Keith and fiddle player Mark O'Connor. After the gig I pressed a cassette of badly-made demos into his hand, instructing him to listen to them as soon as he got a chance. I was expecting a call, sooner rather that later, telling me to jump on a plane. 'I've played the cassette to Willie Nelson. Willie is bowled over, and has decided to cut a half dozen of your songs. He would also like you to be present, just in case there are some lyrical changes he needs to run by you.'

The call never came. Jim listened to the cassette, and having endured the first couple of songs, put it into a very large black bin liner, which contained many hundreds of the same nondescript demos that he received daily.

'Don't send me country songs. Send me your own songs and if they're good, we'll make country songs of 'em. There's a thousand cab-drivers in Nashville writing a country song between fares, and what's more, they all think that they've written a hit.'

As Jim parked his Buick opposite Browne's Diner, I wondered if Philip had given me the right contact after all. We were heading for what seemed to be a large run-down mobile home. Jim was right about the food though: I could smell burger smoke at 30 paces. There was a cheap neon sign saying Browne's Diner over the door and raw wooden steps leading up to it. We pushed the door and entered a no-frills-attached, large version of an Irish shebeen.

'Hey, Rooney, whatcha up to?' said Don Everly.

An Everly Brother in the flesh!

In another life, as I ploughed through my Irish essay on Sunday afternoons, Alan Freeman would tell me that 'Cathy's Clown' had moved to number eight in the charts, and was still climbing, and yes, Pop-pickers, 'here it comes.'

And 'Here he cooooomes, that's Cathy's Clown' would distract me from my *Modh Foshuiteach Caite agus an Tuiseal Ginideach*. The essay would become a *scéal* of two halves. The pristine harmonies would lodge in my brain, and I'd wonder if Cathy was prettier than Mary Larkin from Garryowen who set my heart thumping every time we passed each other. Don and Phil knew about my situation. They spoke to me. They spoke to Mary. They articulated what we couldn't say.

'I'm so lonesome every day,' they sang. They spoke on our behalf: said the things we were unable to say. Our hearts thumped and our faces reddened as we passed each other wordlessly, and waited for 'Hey there, Pop-pickers' on Sundays.

Jim introduced me to Don and his girlfriend Diane, the barman, and a few more of the regulars.

'This here is my friend Mick Hanly. He's over from Ireland. He's a songwriter like the rest of you, but he probably doesn't know exactly where your great-great-granny came from, so give the guy a break. He's also a friend of Donnelly's.'

'Donnelly. Hell, you look far too healthy to be a friend of Donnelly's,' said Don. 'Hey, how's that sonofagun doing? Jeez, I remember . . . .'

A litany of Philip Donnelly anecdotes follows. All amusing, all having gathered mythical moss with retelling.

Being on the dry at the time (one more attempt), I was anxious to buy before anybody got the idea that I didn't drink because I was a skinflint, or that I abhorred alcohol, or that I was not one of the boys.

So I insisted on buying a round, to cope with my fish-out-of-water state of mind.

Diane is fine for the moment, thank you. Jim's is a Bud by the neck, and Don's is a Bud Light by the neck. Glasses don't seem to be the norm.

'Could I have a bottle of Bud, a bottle of Bud Light, and a mineral water, please?'

I'm reminded of home. The barman has noted my presence, but hasn't acknowledged my order. I don't want to be too pushy, but I wonder if he's heard my request.

Next time he passes, I begin to repeat my order. He doesn't let me finish.

'I got you the first time, friend. Whatcha say you wanted with the Buds?'

'A mineral water, please.'

'Water. Whatcha mean water?'

'You know, just an ordinary mineral water?'

'You takin' an aspirin?'

'No. But a glass of water from the tap will do fine, thanks.'

'We don't serve water, friend. This is a bar.'

I hate this. Being an alcoholic is much easier. The charming barman adds another dollop of scorn by calling for Jim's attention across the bar.

'Hey, Rooney. Your friend here is looking for water? Whatcha say he was? IRISH?'

My 'never again' resolve drifts out the window with the burger smoke. My spine is still weasel-thin.

'Look, forget the water, I'll have a draught beer, if you don't mind.'

'You want Bud or Coors?'

'It doesn't matter.'

'Which?'

'Bud will do grand, thanks.'

'Sure, friend.'

We went from Browne's Diner to Jack's Tracks. Happily, this is a recording studio and not another bar. After the lay-off, the few beers were making my eyes shine. Jack's Tracks is on 16th Avenue South, which is where most of the publishing houses in Nashville are situated. It was then the headquarters of the Forerunner Music Group, which was jointly owned by Jim, Allen Reynolds, Mark Miller and Terrell Tye. I was only vaguely aware of Allen Reynolds as a songwriter, but the fruit of his production work with Garth Brooks, Kathy Mathea and Crystal Gayle was everywhere to be seen. Albums that had gone eight-times platinum lined the walls. The additional three- and four-times platinums were stacked on the floor still waiting to be hung.

Jim introduces me to one and all as a friend from Ireland. 'He's also a friend of Philip's.'

'You are? Well hey, Mick, it's good to meet ya. How's that ol' Donnelly doin?'

The hospitality is overwhelming. The smell of success is overwhelming. I have one calling card, besides Philip Donnelly's name, and that is my recently recorded album for the new Ringsend Road Studios, called *All I Remember*. It contains my own version of a song called 'Past the Point of Rescue'. I leave a copy of the album with Terrell, and recommend that she listen to the first track called 'Still Haven't Managed'.

LUCK took care of the rest. She listened, but it was 'Past the Point' she heard as a potential album track for her then-boyfriend, Hal Ketchum. In 1991, Hal was one of the new kids on the block, though he'd already been around the block once before. Nevertheless, he's tall, lean and handsome, with the voice of an angel, and Curb Records intend to tell the world about him.

Jim took me to all his usual haunts and I decided to leave going back on the mineral water until I got home. I did a lot of strolling round. Public transport is virtually non-existent in Nashville, and though it's the business home of country music, it is also known in America for insurance corporations and medical centres. I went to see the Hall of Fame a couple of times. One visit is a visit too many. I have no interest in clothes, and the Hall of Fame has a lot of clothes. Tammy Wynette's dresses. George Jones's elfin suits. Johnny Cash's long, black coats. I move from glass-case to glass-case, rueing the fact that I've parted with ten dollars to look at the wardrobe of country music. There is some light relief. A guitar case, belonging to George Jones, which has been converted to a drinks cabinet. It's compartmentalised to accommodate a bottle and four tumblers. The cover of the case is beautifully hand-painted with the words 'Yesterday's Wine', one of George's many hits. I'm sure that this was the guitar that George insisted on bringing aboard whatever plane he was catching. Were it not for the writer's corner, my ten bucks would have been wasted.

To the non-writer, these pieces of paper are as interesting as a pair of Barbara Mandrell's false eyelashes are to me.

I spot the original text of 'Wolverton Mountain'. I can't take my eyes off it. Here is the first draft of the Claude King hit, which became part of the Hanly household party repertoire in the 60s. 'Sunday Morning Coming Down' is there in Kristofferson's own hand, scratch-outs and inserts, on the original Monument Publishing Company paper. I feel like I'm being allowed a glimpse of some great mystery. But there is no mystery. The hit songwriters do as much chopping and changing as I do. The day before I leave for home I part with another ten bucks to scrutinise them again, and make a mental picture of George's guitar case.

I didn't fancy Nashville too much. If Jim hadn't been such a wonderful host, I'd probably have left after a couple of days, with a plan for a guitar case, and a feeling of bafflement.

I said goodbye to all the guys in Jack's Tracks. Each one told me to 'come back soon, now, and give our regards to Donnelly.' Jim drove me to the airport. I thanked him for his hospitality, and he went back to co-producing Hal Ketchum's first album for Curb with Allen Reynolds. The finished product was released in 1991 and was called *Past the Point of Rescue*.

Publishers don't usually inform songwriters that their song has been cut until the record comes to hand, and songwriters don't usually believe them until they receive the record. This is to save the publisher having to impart the bad news, that despite the fact that the artist cut the song, the producer decided at the last moment that it did not fit the picture, and that the song had been dropped.

Jim and Terrell went out on a limb to tell me that Curb had earmarked 'Past the Point' as the third single from the album. This meant that they were hoping that the first two singles would generate enough interest, and chart high enough to take the title track to No. 1. Hal's first single from the album, a song called 'Small Time Saturday Night', and Hal's own 'I Know Where Love Lives', were both top-ten records, and confidence was high at Forerunner that 'Past the Point' would take the No. 1 spot in Billboard. It never did. It made all the right moves and was destined for the No. 1 spot, but Billy Ray Cyrus released 'Achy Breaky Heart' and all hell broke loose. He went to No. 1 in the space of four weeks. (Normally they plan for an eight-week campaign to take a song to No. 1.) 'Past the Point' had to settle for second place. Nevertheless, it became the most played BMI country song in America for 1993. In 1994 it passed the one-million-radio-plays mark, joining songs such as 'Wonderful Tonight', 'Sledgehammer', 'As Tears Go By' and 'Lola'. In 2002, it passed the two-million-radio-plays mark.

In October 1994 BMI held the award ceremony in the Dorchester Hotel in London. Marie and I put on our finery and went to join McCartney, Morrison, Seal and Stevie Winwood, who were also on the awards list and were there in the flesh. I was overwhelmed to be in such exalted company. I introduced myself to Bruce Welch, rhythm guitarist with The Shadows and told him about the difference that hearing 'Apache' for the first time had made to my life. He wasn't all that interested. He was drinking orange juice; I was drinking champagne, and definitely the more talkative. Also, I was probably the millionth person who'd told him the same story.

In 1991, my royalty statements were still the dribbles that make your yearly visit to the guardian of your overdraft a penance. 'I've written a great song' doesn't mean much to a banker who doesn't want to stop looking at the computer screen, for fear that the look in his/her eyes betray the fact that they think you're a nut, or someone who's looking for a free lunch.

In October 1992, my quarterly cheque from the Performing Rights Society came to £1,139.32 sterling. In April it came to £842.39.

No cigar this Christmas either.

Two days before Christmas, the December payout arrived. £2,923.69.

Yippee! Saved.

Collect the turkey. After a celebratory glass, I pick up the royalty printout to see which songs are doing the business. At the bottom of the statement I notice an extra zero after the two. It can't be. But it is. 'Past the Point of Rescue' has kicked in. I examine the cheque again. £20,923.69 smackeroos. It's for real. I throw my arms around Marie and tell her to order two turkeys. We've hit pay-dirt. I've written a song that has made me twenty grand richer, and ex-Prime Minister, Charles Haughey, in an inspired moment, has decreed that I can hold on to it all. I've written something that is deemed 'to be original and of artistic merit' and the royalties gained are tax-free. I want to call the bank and say 'I told you it was a good song,' but I opt for lodging the cheque and let them work it out for themselves. The dribble has suddenly become a flood, and Christmas is celebrated with great relief.

More than that, my *raison d'être* had been verified. (Back then I was far more certain that I merited the title 'Songwriter' than I do now, but without commercial success self-doubt becomes a debilitating factor, even for the most confident.) Now I had a gold calling-card. There wasn't a writer in Nashville who didn't think that 'Past the Point' was a good song. It had a freshness, and was not written to formulae. However, there was a problem. I didn't consider myself to be a writer of country songs. I loved good country music. I still do. Ten per cent of it is wonderful, but just like pop music the other 90 per cent is disposable trash. When Hal Ketchum had his success with 'Past the Point', country music was in a state of flux. Garth Brooks had become a worldwide phenomenon. He had achieved the cross-over and moved into Neil Diamond territory. Big shows. Big sales. Big bucks. Big hats. Major record labels were lining up a potential new 'Garth' every month and releasing their first albums with a fanfare announcing the newest country sensation. If the album didn't do the business that the accountants could live with, then the option on the second album wasn't taken up. The young singer had his fifteen minutes in the spotlight. He then spent the rest of his career in the dark, hawking his hit from tavern to tavern, singing it to ever-diminishing crowds of the faithful. I didn't feel that I wrote songs in that mould and, despite the success of 'Past the Point', didn't want to change my *modus operandi.*

Over the next couple of years I became good friends with Hal and Terrell, and they invited me to their home in Nashville to try to co-write some songs with Hal. We didn't write much but we talked a lot, and I enjoyed their company. Over dinner one evening, Hal mentions another song from the *All I Remember* album that has taken his fancy. The song is

'Fall Like a Stone'. It's a tongue-in-cheek love song. It's very over-the-top and contains the lines:

'I'm gonna fall like a stone, I'm gonna break every bone
I'm gonna bounce all my cheques, in cheap discothèques
'til my body lies prone'

'I can really dig that "Fall Like a Stone", maybe I should take a shot at it,' says Hal.

'Aw, I don't know, honey, I'm not so sure that it would suit you.'

'But why not?'

Terrell puts her finger on the word 'discothèque'.

'I'm not sure that the radio people would get it. We don't use the word discothèque these days. Maybe. Well . . . I don't know.'

Discothèque was a no-no for Terrell, whose job it was to be tuned into these things. Being the sweetheart that she is, she was being polite to me because I wasn't in the Forerunner stable of songwriters: had I been, she would have instructed me to come up with a different word, before she'd start pitching the song. It was a revealing moment.

There are many other limitations for the Nashville song-writer, and one of the cardinal rules is: You don't portray your star in a bad light.

He can be so lonesome, he could cry, and he can stay lonesome until verse three, ''cause she's never comin' back'.

He can be drunk, and stay drunk until he falls down in verse three, ''cause she's never comin' back'.

He can be empty, crippled, heartbroken, cryin' blind, losin' his mind, desperate, ''cause she's never comin' back'.

Your average blue-collar worker, nursing his pitcher, iden-
tifies with this man. He is this man. He's been down that road
and if he can't sort out his problem with Lucinda when he gets
home, hell, he'll be goin' down that road again. Jeez, this Mark
Chestnut guy is talkin' to me. Damn good song that.

'*It's too hot for golf, but it's too cold at home.*'

The woman in her skin-tight jeans and embroidered denim
shirt recognises that man.

'I could fix him, if only he'd let me,' she thinks.

The only thing your star is not allowed to say is 'I'm
frightened.' If he does, he'd better have it sorted by verse
three or he's a loser, and nobody wants to part with 30 bucks
to see a loser. Men can't be frightened in country music. They
can fear the Lord but nothing else.

I relate the Nashville experience, because people often ask
me why I didn't haunt the Nashville publishing houses with
my 'gold card', following the success of 'Past the Point'. The
answer is, for better or worse, I plough my own furrow. If Paul
Simon can pass through Saginaw, Michigan in song, I feel I
should be able to pass through Kildorrery, Co. Limerick. If he
can mention the Mississippi Delta, then I should be able to
mention Plassey River. If he can compare the Mississippi
Delta to a National Guitar, then I should be able to say that
the only gun I owned 'was a hurling stick'. Not many people
in Boise, Ohio will have heard of a hurling stick, but then not
many people in Kildorrery will have heard of a National
Guitar either. Neither community is diminished by this fact,
but I feel that the mention of the words 'hurling stick' in a
good song would not bother your average Joe in Boise, any
more than National Guitar bothers Paul Simon fans in
Kildorrery. But it does bother the movers and shakers in
Nashville, so the citizens of Boise never get to ask the question:

'What is a hurling stick?' Whether this gap in Joe's education is in fact a loss or not is a question I can't answer.

Following the success of 'Past the Point', the professional songwriter would have gone back to the drawing board and sifted through the ingredients that made it a hit song, put them in the blender, and spat out the follow-up, hoping the result would be similar enough to remind the punter of the hit and make them want more of the same. If he was trying to earn a living solely from his song-writing, the ingredients of 'I Am, I Am' might cross his mind but would never see the light of day as a song. Happily, I have the safety net of being a performer, and if the sheriff comes knocking I can throw my hat on the pavement and start strumming. I know that there won't be a queue of singers waiting to get their hands on 'I Am, I Am' and go rushing to the nearest studio to record it. If someone has the temerity to try, his or her producer will probably say,

'You can't sing that. *"I am, I am, I'm frightened 'cause I am."* What the hell are you frightened of? Who do you think you are? Mick Hanly?'

I think that being frightened is a legitimate subject for a song, and 'I Am, I Am' is on *Wish Me Well* because it describes a feeling that I get from time to time.

Sometimes I'm afraid.

Sometimes I'm terrified.

Sometimes, when I'm driving at night, I have to turn on the light and check that there isn't a bogeyman in the back seat.

Most of the time I'm not afraid. Most of the time I'm not terrified. Most of the time I'm capable, and in control. But my fears and insecurities drove me to drink, to smoke, and take any drug I could get my hands on, except heroin. And it was fear didn't allow me to touch heroin.

In the song 'All I Remember', I sing: *'I'm not the one that you see.'*
  In 'The Crusader', I sing *'This is me, facing me.'*
  At 54 years of age I feel that I need to sing it again:
  'I'm frightened 'cause I am.'

Note: In May 2004 I emailed my final manuscript amend-
ments to my editor in Gill & Macmillan. They were mostly
factual corrections that, for the sake of continuity, I'd allowed
to go unchecked in the course of the writing. I'd gone
through the correction process as diligently as I could, and
when it was done, I was glad to see the back of it. For a songwriter, the gestation period of a book, even as short as this
one, is two years too long. I was aching for closure, but a
detail in the foregoing chapter began to haunt me.

Was 'Achy Breaky Heart' the song that kept 'Past the Point
of Rescue' from reaching the number one spot in May 1992?
I had a lingering suspicion that this piece of information was
an off-the-cuff quip from a past live performance which now,
through overuse, was parading itself as fact? Casting the
much-maligned 'Achy Breaky Heart' in the role of spoilsport
is a cheap shot. I take full responsibility for it, though
it could have come from a smartass in the audience whose
standards were as low as my own. I decided to check it at
source. After several inquiries to Billboard Research Services
in New York, I uncovered the following:

'Past the Point of Rescue' went to No. 2 in the Billboard
Hot Country Singles charts in the week ending 9 May 1992.
The No. 1 song for that week was 'Neon Moon' by Brooks &
Dunn. 'Past The Point' was No. 2 for one week only and then
started to descend. On that particular week, 'Achy Breaky
Heart' was No. 17 and climbing.

I Am, I Am

Verse 1
Are you ever tempted when you're driving home
And the big truck goes thundering past
To give the steering wheel one twist
And make that sudden twist your last
Go from being heaven's gift
To bastard traitor overnight
Leave the ones you've goodbye kissed
To cry forever.

Chorus
I am, I am, I'm frightened 'cause I am
I am, I am, I'm frightened 'cause I am.

Verse 2
I saw the Cliffs of Moher once
They seemed to sing a siren's song
I heard the seagulls crying too
I backed away, moved along
I pay my fare for the Eiffel Tower
The view takes your breath away
Don't know why I'm drawn back down
To watch the river.

Chorus

Verse 3

I love my wife and kids much more
Than anything I'll ever write
So you can clap 'til the cows come home
Can't wait to kiss them all tonight
I'm not going anywhere
And I don't know why I'm tempted to
Gaze into the great abyss
Stand and shiver.

Chorus

Two-turkey Christmas! First five-figure cheque from the Performing Rights Society

BMI awards in the Dorchester Hotel. 'Past the Point of Rescue' passes the one-million-radio-plays mark in the US

GOLD & GOLD WORLD

COLD, COLD WORLD

When I was a child, the site on which the University of Limerick now stands was green pasture. Plassey House stood alone and aloof in the middle of the green fields and looked down on Plassey River, that part of the Shannon above Limerick City. The name Plassey is derived from the palas tree or 'flame of the forest' which, in turn, gave its name to a village in India. Robert Clive, the son of a Shropshire squire, led an army to a decisive victory at the Battle of Plassey. In 1760, at the age of 34, he returned to England in ill-health, and was given a scattered Irish estate in Limerick and Co. Clare. Thus Clive became Baron of Plassey, and the district was renamed after its new owner.

The early view of the river from the house would have been a fine one. Immediately, you would have seen the sturdy Black Bridge and the tall mill beside it. Above that was the Garrison Wall and a white-water stretch where fisherman, out from the city on their bikes, would quietly cast their salmon fly daily.

Beyond was countryside for as far as the eye could see, to the Clare hills. By the time we started to swim, this vista would have been obscured by the now-mature trees that lined the bank from the end of the white water, stretching for another half-mile along the riverbank.

My father used to ferry us in his Morris Minor to outside the churchyard, behind the Hurler's Bar, where he reluctantly parked. If he could have driven it as far as the bank, he would have — in fact, if he could have gone swimming in the car, he would have, he was that fond of it. From the church we went on foot through the university campus, then green fields, to our swimming hole. Many a summer's evening we spent diving from our reed-built platform into the brown shallows. We weren't bothered by the murkiness, for which the cattle cooling themselves upstream were responsible, nor the flies which annoyed my father so much. We jack-knifed and sky-dived like tumbler pigeons, and we pushed and jostled for a place on the platform like hungry calves at a bucket. Every half-hour we brought the deflated car-tube back to my father for a pump, and fought over it until it no longer supported us. No matter how long we spent in the swim, the order to pack up was always greeted with protest,

'Can we have one more dive, Dad?'

'One more so, let ye, and we'll be off.'

With our hair sticking up like crested cockatoos, we traipsed back to the Morris Minor, dragging our towels, los-ing our togs, fought in the back seat of the Morris as our legs stuck to the sweating leather, fell into bed and deep slumber.

In 1963, Plassey River froze over. On the night of 24 January the temperature dropped to 24 degrees below freezing. It was the beginning of the coldest snap of the century and it lasted from the end of December right into March. In Limerick, for the first time in living memory, the Shannon could be crossed dry-footed from the shore at Corbally to St

Thomas's Island, and the Abbey River at Athlunkard Boat Club was an ice floe stretching almost halfway across. Arctic conditions prevailed throughout the city and county. St Patrick's Road, where I lived, did not escape unscathed.

On the road, our neighbours were more or less normal, but, for an assortment of reasons, there were exceptions. Some people 'suffered from their nerves'. This was a polite catch-all phrase for agoraphobics, depressives, eccentrics and anyone else who was odd. There were also martyrs, who were too fond of the drink, and saints, who were too fond of their prayers.

The Malones were just such an exception, not because Mrs Malone was suffering from her nerves, though she had every right to be, but because Mr Malone was dour, sullen and an alcoholic. There were also other factors, the principal one being the wretched poverty in which they lived. Their house was a run-down cottage, with front and back gardens gone to wilderness. Nothing was ever repaired or replaced. The bottom planks of the front door were rotting and looked like a mouthful of jagged teeth. Loosened roof-tiles lodged precariously in the gutters, and window panes were repaired with cardboard. The front door knocker was stiff from lack of use.

There were three Malone children. An older girl, whom I remember only vaguely and who disappeared to England as soon as her age would allow, a younger brother Jim, who followed quickly after, and the youngest girl, Lettie, who needed special care.

Despite her circumstances, Mrs Malone was a gregarious and friendly woman. She made every effort to put on a show with the meagre resources at her disposal. Her silvery-grey hair was coiffed daily and the resulting construction was kept in place with a pair of combs. She never left the house without her overcoat, which had buttons the size of tennis-balls, and the hem of which was sometimes at half-mast. It was below the hem that poverty's secret was revealed. In summer, cheap canvas shoes and no socks; in winter, cheap canvas shoes, a pair of her husband's socks and rosy chilblains.

What went on in the mind of the demented Jim is impossible to know. What great disappointment had him daily reaching for copious doses of drink? It was only ever alluded to at home in the context of the weight of Mrs Malone's cross.

Three nights before the temperature dropped to its lowest, the water froze in our pipes. My father had wrapped them in sacking, but to no avail. The same was true up and down the road. The only exception was the Malone cottage. One day, on the gossip trail, Mrs Malone announced, by the way, that she was blessed and that 'thanks be to God', their tap hadn't frozen. Before the day's end, word of a lively trickle at Malones had reached every household on the road and what began as a tentative, polite stream of visitors, quickly became an invasion. Within 24 hours the trip to the cottage for a couple of buckets of precious water became a daily staple.

We came with an assortment of vessels. Buckets that were used to hold the soiled nappies were scalded and press-ganged into a more noble calling; sweet tins that were normally used to fetch the milk in the morning, or blackberries in the summer; cooking pots that spilled half the contents before one got home. The door with the jagged teeth began to wobble with overuse, so Mrs Malone left it slightly ajar, despite the cold.

The Malones' home was turned upside down. Never had the cottage seen such traffic. Even the unpredictability of Jim's presence didn't stem the tide; he became more invisible. He was never in the kitchen when the throng invaded his home, but Mrs Malone relished her new role.

'Don't mind the state of the place, Mrs Sheehan, I didn't get a chance to take the sweeping brush to it yet, with all the visitors, God help us.'

'Don't be standing over there in the draught, Michael, isn't it? Come in here and warm your hands.'

Lettie told me that I had lovely curls, and tried to touch them. Mrs Malone buzzed and sparkled. She apologised again and again for 'the state of the place' to the callers who were forced to queue and couldn't be seated, or who felt uncomfortable, who asked would she mind if they left the buckets (they'd call on their way back from the Novena). Her star rose. While the world froze, her neighbours thawed, and she thrived on being inside the circle. She was just getting used to the company when the carousel suddenly stopped.

One morning when we woke up everything was dripping. The copper pipe over the hot-press had burst and every clean sheet and tablecloth we possessed became saturated. The plumber, Paddy Rockett, had to come and replace the pipe, which looked as though it had been opened with a can-opener. Outside, we could lift our feet again. By the time I got to the Black Bridge, all trace of the ice had disappeared. A few brown, and black, feathered corpses lay on the bank, and the assortment of stones that had littered the ice had glided silently to the bottom of the river.

Mrs Malone's star also glided silently to earth to resume its former position in the community galaxy. She had exposed her wretchedness to the world with a will, and received nothing in return. She was prepared to love her neighbour. What she got in return was her neighbour's tolerance.

Cold, Cold World

Verse 1
When Plassey froze over the ice was like stone
And no one had water but Mrs Malone
So we trooped to her gate with our buckets and cans
Suddenly she was our neighbour.

Verse 2
Normally nobody darkened her door
'Cause Mrs Malone was poorer than poor
Jim was her husband and not a nice man
But his was the house with the water.

Verse 3
And there in the kitchen as the buckets filled up
We turned a blind eye to poverty's work
Now centre stage she was smiling and kind
While Jim went to fume in the bedroom.

Verse 4
She said 'the front door is open to all
Sure there's never a lock on that front door at all'
And it wasn't too long before people presumed
To let themselves in without knocking.

Verse 5
For five weeks we dropped bric-a-bric-bric-a-brac
From the Black Bridge on Plassey but the ice wouldn't crack
While the tap in the kitchen kept spilling the gold
And Mrs Malone was the hostess.

Verse 6

Jim drank his quota and he fumed a lot more
His dragon's breath hissed through the cracks in the door
While Mrs Malone became queen of the road
And started to dream in the process.

Verse 7

She dreamed Mrs Murphy was coming to tea
That Jim held her hand as they walked by the sea
She dreamed she had money, she dreamed she had hopes
She dreamed she could buy herself stockings.

Verse 8

And then without warning the cold snap was done
And the ice started breaking with the sound of a gun
We fixed all the leaks, threw the buckets aside
And went back to keeping our distance.

Verse 9

The procession over the silence returned
Her gentle entreaties were carelessly spurned
And all we, her neighbours, could think of to say
Was 'Mrs Malone, only for you'.

Verse 10

But she waited and waited, she waited in vain
And the beautiful dreams disappeared in the rain
Then one day Jim dropped his paper and said
'I'm glad we're rid of those fuckers.'

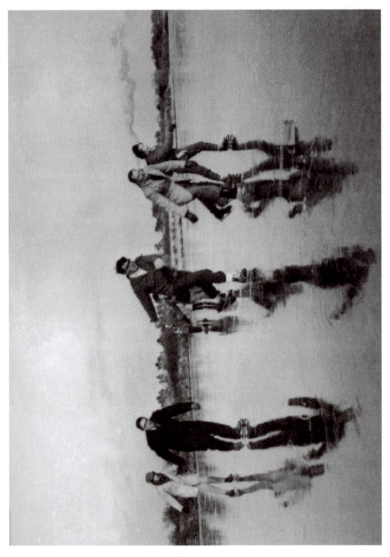

The Big Freeze, Limerick 1963 (Photo: courtesy of Sean Curtin)

'Off the ice, Maggie' (Photo: courtesy of Sean Curtin)

WISH ME WELL

I stopped drinking alcohol on 21 March 2001. After 30 years of trying to get it right, I finally gave up. Of all the things I've done, despite endless hours of practice, my drinking was the one thing that disimproved. The more practice I put in the worse I got. Whiskey was my mugger; it crept up on me and hit me with a cosh over the head. By the time I stopped, there were four to five litre-and-a-half bottles of Paddy coming into the house, per week, and I was drinking 95 per cent of it. The ordinary household bottle of Paddy was not fat enough, not golden enough, and not long-lasting enough, to serve my needs. It emptied far too quickly. It reminded me of my consumption too often for comfort. The litre-and-a-half bottle, designed for a bar with average consumption, was far more comforting since, having emptied half of it, there was still a half-bottle left for tomorrow, and if I didn't finish that at a sitting, it could be made to look as if it had lasted three whole days; not the kind of consumption that would have your heart specialist clapping you on the back, but, to my foggy brain, not alarming. But it still wasn't enough. A dog with a mallet up his arse would have realised that he was losing the mind games with the whiskey bottle, but not me. This dog thought that the mallet was a bone that he wouldn't release for love nor money. Eventually, love won.

When I finally went over the cliff and hit the rocks below, Marie was saying to me, 'I can't live with this, Michael, I can't live with this.' These were the tough words of love that she was reduced to. 'I can't live with this': they were also the words that I'd been longing to hear. I was relieved to be given an ultimatum.

Despite the fact that I was deeply unhappy about the way I was drinking, about the fact that it was an awful tyranny in my life, about the distance it was placing between my loved ones and me, I still refused to stop. In fact, the determination with which I was trying to self-destruct staggers me today as much as drink ever did, two and a half years later. It still makes no sense to me. I have a lovely home, a wonderful family, a beautiful, caring and loving wife; we all have our health, our fingers, our toes and our senses; we're blessed; I'm blessed. Yet, there I was, trying my best to bring it all crashing down on top of us.

Since stopping, I've had to make way for a lot of emotional turmoil, which bubbled to the surface now that the lid was off. After the initial euphoria of goals reached — one month, two months, six months, a year — the counting stopped and the reckoning began. There is no shortage of stuff there from my childhood which is extremely painful for me to recall: beatings and humiliations which caused me deep hurt. Betrayals and abandonments, imagined and real, which stung me to the quick, and left me with a deep distrust of authority. Overall, a sense of fear, which pervaded my whole growing up; a sense that I wasn't lovable, or worth loving, and that I'd better start juggling balls, or hurling out of my skin, or strumming a guitar, because I had nothing else to offer.

If I had started to drink manically late in my life, I might be able to say that the reason was that 30 years of insecurity and rakishness had finally caught up with me, and I was crying in my beer, but I drank manically from day one. I never drank because I was thirsty, or for taste, or for fun. I drank to get pissed. And if I didn't get pissed, I got cranky: felt disappointed, and cheated. Where does this insatiability come from? And why can't a half-litre of whiskey fill it? Why wouldn't a litre of whiskey fill it? What would it take to fill it? Is it fillable?

I recently read an interview with Nick Nolte, in which he said that the 'shout stop' mechanism in his brain doesn't work, and that he doesn't know when he has had enough of anything. When I was drinking, I knew more often than not when I'd had enough: I heard the word stop, but I didn't stop. I never deliberately set out to black out, but I did it every time I got the chance. Reports that I was actually fine during moments that escaped my recollection, all helped to bolster an increasingly fragile armour, but I knew the truth was different, and that these reports were from sources who were only slightly less pissed than myself.

I had a normal childhood. My parents were good people. They sacrificed, scrimped, saved, went without, that we might have better than they. I was never hungry or cold. I was never ill-clad. My father and my mother weren't china-breaking or fist-fighting alcoholics, or deserters, or sexual abusers. So why was I trying to kill myself at 50?

One thing that I really disliked about drink was the tyranny of it, but before we get to that, let me tell you what I loved about it.

I got drunk for the first time when I was about 20. I was at a dance in Young Munster's Rugby Club in Limerick. Dances were necessary evils as far as I was concerned. I didn't know how to dance and was as terrified of asking a girl to dance as she was of not being asked. Surprisingly, for a musician, I'm painfully awkward and have no physical rhythm. On this particular night I had three bottles of Carlsberg Special and suddenly I was Rudolf Nureyev. I took off. It was the most beautiful moment of abandon that I'd ever experienced. I couldn't believe that my tongue-tied, crippling gaucheness could be banished so easily. Some of the onlookers were amused, though nobody was impressed. But most importantly, I didn't care. It was the most exhilarating moment of my life to date, and I wouldn't have missed it for all the Carlsberg Special in Kilkenny.

I've had many similar moments over the years, but they never had that same liberating effect, because they were now being governed by my efforts at trying, not to be a flapping butterfly, but a cool Steve McQueen as well.

I've never taken heroin — never had the courage — but I'm told that the first hit is the biggest one that you'll ever have, and that the rest of your addiction is spent trying to recapture the first rush; hence chasing the dragon. I spent all my drinking years trying to regain that Carlsberg Special moment. I didn't succeed, but I came close enough, often enough, to keep me trying and I nearly killed myself in the process.

A pint of Guinness was my drink. Sitting with my third pint of the day, a packet of Players Navy Cut, and a ten-pound note in my pocket was my idea of heaven. I was affected by a touch of butterfly and a hint of Steve McQueen. I found myself witty, interesting, irresistible. Bring on the girls, the professors, my fellow musicians and poets: I'll talk to you all. I'm in the comfort zone. Listen to me! I'm interesting. I've something to say. I'm worth loving.

I loved that window of time. I loved it every time I drank. It was always as good as the time before, and up to the day I stopped, it still hadn't lost its glow. It got shorter, the faster I drank, but I kept chasing it, always believing that I was going to stay in the moment, but never doing so. Sometimes, I miss that romp in the meadow, and, if I could have just that, I'd start drinking again in the morning. But, in order to have that romp I have to negotiate so many briars and mud-holes, on the way to and from the mirage, that it's no longer worth it. I have yet to find another way into the meadow. The search continues.

There's something beautiful about sitting outside a bar in any town in the world and nursing the local speciality. There's also something very attractive about sitting in one's own back garden, gazing at the view, if you have one, or surveying the potato drills you've just dug, or the wall that you've just built. It's reward time. Your bones are aching slightly, but it's enjoyable aching because it's as a result of work that you've done for yourself; you're about to get pleasantly pissed, and all is well with the world.

From time to time, Marie says to me, 'I'd love if you could have a glass of wine with me,' and I say, 'yea, that would be nice.' It's a simple wish on both our parts; a simple sharing of one of the riches of man's harvesting; a little ceremonial act, enhancing our togetherness; a tipping of glasses; a smile; a 'just us' moment.

For now, it's a moment that will have to wait, and the wait could be a long one. I'm beginning to lose interest in these mirages. It happened me too when I stopped smoking and I suspect that for alcohol, the same process has already begun.

I stopped smoking in 1984. I used to smoke John Players Navy Cut, and by the time I gave them up, they had become a tyranny in my life. I couldn't pick up the guitar without lighting a cigarette. I couldn't get on a bus without climbing the stairs to join my fellow addicts. I couldn't have a cup of tea, drink a pint, read the paper, open a book, make a phone call. In fact, the only time that I didn't smoke was when I was asleep. To make matters worse, most of the time I wasn't even enjoying them. I resented the tyranny more than anything, but, as with the drink, the thoughts of stopping presented a vista so appalling that I couldn't make the leap. By the time I stopped, there were just two parts of my day left when I could say that I enjoyed a cigarette. One was a period of a couple of hours after my lunch, and the other was my drinking hours. In the morning after the customary hawking and hacking was done, the first seven or eight cigarettes were smoked without pleasure. I could sense my body saying, 'please don't subject me to another day of this.'

I heard, but I couldn't respond. Approaching lunch-hour, the clamour subsided and I started to approach the pleasure zone. It was as though my body was saying, 'sorry about that jittery rush, but I'm OK now, so let's enjoy.' After my lunch, I always had a cup of tea and a cigarette. Now came the great chorus from the hold, 'sure life wouldn't be worth living if you couldn't have an oul smoke.'

By four o'clock in the afternoon, I felt burnt out. That feeling did not prevent the addition of a brand new, cellophane-wrapped pack of John Players to the shopping basket. As my throat grew rawer and rawer as the late afternoon progressed, hours of drinking lay ahead, so the pleasure zone could be revisited, the intake increased in direct ratio to drink consumption, the rawness forgotten, all moderation abandoned, until it was hawking and hacking time again.

I lay in bed one morning with a severe flu, an empty Paddy bottle which had held the contents of the makings of ten stiff hot whiskeys that had been consumed for medicinal purposes, a half-jar of honey, a bowl containing 25 spent lemon slices, which had been daggered with cloves, and five cigarettes remaining in a 20-John-Players box. I felt like a shit on a slate, so I lit my first cigarette of the day. I won't describe the next hour. Even at this remove, it's too much for my stomach to take, but I had crossed the Rubicon necessary for stopping. It didn't happen for another six months, but the mental conditioning necessary to kick the habit was put in train. I set a date.

As with any addiction, there's never a suitable time to stop. There's always something — Christmas, St Patrick's Day, the All-Ireland Hurling Final, an anniversary that you've forgotten. Despite the fact that, at the time, I was haunted by my failure with the band, Moving Hearts, my break-up with my first wife Úna, my weekly visit to the dole office, I chose this moment to stop. As I said, it's never easy, and there's never a good time, and 1984 was not a good year for Mick Hanly, yet, for some reason, giving up smoking felt like a positive thing to do rather than a further deprivation.

I did something else, which I found helpful. I'm not much different from Pavlov's dog — I wag my tail when I'm given something — so I decided to reward myself for quitting. I spotted two watercolours in the Bank of Ireland in Fairview that I liked. They were by a painter called Tom Daly from Raheny. They were very simple watercolours of the *Miranda Guinness* docked in Dublin Port: yes, the very ship that brought my favourite tipple, and of Findlaters Church in Dublin. There was a price tag of £40 apiece on them. I was getting only £42-something a week in the dole office, but I decided to give myself a present of the two pictures with my saved cigarette money. I informed the teller at the bank that I wanted to buy the pictures. She didn't wait for me to tell her that I had no money and that I needed to do a deal with the artist, and that I could only pay ten bob a week . . .

She came back with two red stickers on top of two of her fingers.

'Which two did you say again?'

'Well, hold on a second, can you give me your man's address?'

'Oh . . . I see. What will I do with these?' she asked.

I was tempted to tell her, but said nothing.

Tom's address was on the back of one of the paintings. I contacted him, and he agreed to let me buy them by instalments. They're the first two pictures that you see as you come through our front door.

I also did something else, which I found helpful; I stopped smoking joints. I know that you're laughing, and that you never heard of anything so ridiculous in your life, but one pull of a joint was the rock on which I foundered on all previous occasions. It's obvious, to those who wish to see, that a joint is just a re-rolled cigarette, with some extra carcinogenic added, but a determined addict can be blind to anything. I'd stick to just joints for a period, but all the time I'd be rolling more and more of them for the tobacco hit. So they had to go by the board, and when they did I continued to smoke hash under a glass, in a pipe; I ate it; if I could have snorted it, I would. Eventually, it became so irksome that I lost interest.

The initial euphoria of having stopped smoking tobacco wore off soon enough, and I got down to the dour business of going without, while a thousand voices whispered, 'sure, they can't be as bad for you as you thought, and aren't you feeling great, and sure one cigarette never did anyone any harm, and don't you deserve something, and . . . .'

The milestones went by slowly, painfully, at first. It seemed as if I spent my days thinking of nothing else but of trying not to think about cigarettes. The 'could get run over by a truck' argument raised its illogical head more often than ever. But the hawking and hacking stopped, the pictures were hung, the days turned into months and I started to lose interest in the count. After a year, I felt that I had left the danger zone, but I had developed a loathsome sense of moral superiority towards my fellow addicts. In fact, I didn't regard them as my fellow anything anymore. They were the lost and the damned. The weak, and the polluted, and the polluting. Happily, this feeling of moral superiority hasn't lasted.

I've half-promised myself a glass of golden Black Bush Whiskey with Marie, some summer's evening when the sun is sinking, when all albums are done, all books are written, all children happily flown, and all that mullarky. I have an awful feeling that I won't be able to keep my promise, and that this wistful, dream-like scenario is going to go the same way as the postprandial cigarette. I don't like letting this idea go; a part of it appeals to me — it's probably the Black Bush part. I read an interview with Eric Clapton, in which he said that he missed 'the pint of bitter, outside the Cock and Chicken, on a summer's afternoon, while the cricket ball clacked on the town common', or words to that effect. He thought that it was a very English, and a very special, thing. I know what he's talking about. I could bring you to Thurles and show you the Irish equivalent on Munster Hurling Final day. It is very special and it holds huge appeal. The vomited steak and chips, the car accident, the fall down the stairs, the bitter row with wife or partner: they never appeared in the same frame, and no matter how many times that I'd seen it, I found it impossible to run the whole movie in my head.

I'm on my way, so wish me well. Alcohol had become a dictator in my life. It ran the show; it doesn't anymore. Of course I miss it. Of course I miss the taking off, the Carlsberg Special moments. I miss the looseness, the banter, the laughter, sometimes even the madness. I miss meeting the local fraternity and hearing the gospel; the real reason why a Mullally or a Fennelly has been sidelined; why there hasn't been a fish caught all season; who's robbing whom; the one that came from the horse's mouth; all that song-writing material that requires hours of listening and research! I miss the reward system that I'd developed for a good day at the office, or a good day in the garden, or on the building site. I called it 'relaxing with a couple of pints'; the great golden depth-charges of Paddy that went with them weren't mentioned, and I always gave myself my reward whether I went to the office or not. Alcohol can be wonderful, and I'd give my eye-teeth to be able to handle it, but I can't. End of story.

Of course it's not the end of the story. At the moment I don't miss alcohol enough to bother going back on it, and as time goes by, I feel that I'll be less and less interested. There are too many pluses in my life as a result of its absence, and they outweigh the minuses by a ton. I can go to gigs and plays and movies and remember what I've seen and heard. I can go to dinner with friends and not fall asleep in the vegetable serving. I can drive where and when I like and can commit myself to driving somebody, somewhere, sometime, without worrying. These are just a few of the positives; there are a million more.

Most importantly, as I climb the stairs to bed every night, I can hear Ellen's voice saying:

'Is that you, Dad? Will you say goodnight to me?'

Wish Me Well

Verse 1
It's time to start out on a brand new run
Sort out the debris, lay down that gun
How many times must I hear that bell?

Verse 2
Don't know for certain if I'm strong enough
But I'm the one who wants to call my bluff
Blow the door off this prison cell.

Chorus
I love you dearly, you love me too
Reassured, I make the moves I do
All I could see when the blindfold fell was
You still waiting, you still waiting
You still waiting, to wish me well.

Verse 3
It's time to bury some of these old songs
They've had their day but now their day is gone
They clog my pockets like broken shell.

Verse 4
The truth's not easy and the tears are slow
Sometimes too painful for those tears to flow
Hold my hand, because flow they will.

Chorus

Verse 5
There's a golden child somewhere, wide-eyed
I hear his voice across the great divide
Crying 'mother, don't tell, don't tell.'

Chorus

Jessie and me, Fairview, Dublin 1985 (Photo: Christine Bond)

Katie and Ellen with cone

Happy birthday, Thomas!

THE CRUSADER

Thirteen, Fairgreen, Limerick, was the address of the house where my first wife, Úna, and I began our short marriage together. It was my grandmother's house. Grandmother lived alone, and I asked if we could use the back bedroom of the two-up, two-down until such time as we found a place of our own. I didn't mention the use of the kitchen, the toilet and the garden. There was no bathroom and the coal-shed had been converted into a toilet. Having heat was considered to be far more of a necessity than relieving oneself indoors, when the house was built. I put a glasshouse in the garden for my grass-plants, and promised both my mother, and grandmother, a share of the tomato crop. She often wondered why there were no tomatoes on view, suggesting that I wasn't feeding them properly, since 'Paddy Flynn's plants were already weighed down with fruit.'

We could not afford a place of our own. I had little money, sometimes none; I was jobless, penniless, homeless and futureless. At the time, Úna was eighteen and I was 28, going on seventeen.

For Úna, the move to Limerick after her marriage to me was traumatic. We'd been living in a squalid flat in Sandymount, Dublin, and when one of the upstairs tenants put his foot through our bedroom ceiling, we decided that it was time to move out. I suggested that we go live in the country. Úna could rear ducks and chickens and I'd grow potatoes and build a dovecote, and we could sit around a nice log fire in the cold winter evenings and talk to each other. This hair-brainedness came out on my first night home from a tired-and-emotional six-week tour of Europe, and to round off the scheme, I threw in 'sure, let's get married as well.' So we did, in the University Church on St Stephen's Green, with Úna's father, the novelist Gerry Hanley, her sister Luarena, and my brother Seán as witnesses. The five of us had dinner in the Pheasant Restaurant, near Trinity College, and I played a concert that night in Liberty Hall, still in my wedding best. Úna didn't have to change her name and I felt a country song coming on.

We piled all our earthly goods into my second-hand Renault 4, and decamped for a life in the country, stopping off for a year at my grandmother's house in Limerick. Suddenly, Úna had a new circle of close friends that she hadn't bargained for. My mother and my grandmother, two women well-versed in the ways of childrearing, were in constant and close attendance. When Úna became pregnant with our only daughter, Jessie, they began to knit as though she were expecting triplets. All meant in the kindest possible way, but for the new mother-to-be, hard to take.

In the wings I was watching and not seeing, and listening with only half an ear. I was comfortable living in an ether of self-delusion, into which I believed, any day now, the man with the big cigar was going to step and deliver me. I had recorded three albums: one, with my friend Mícheál Ó Domhnaill, a gifted singer-guitarist, which was called *Celtic Folkweave*, and two more solo efforts for the Mulligan label. I suspect that today I'm probably over-critical of these works. I never listen to them, and if I happen to hear a track by accident, I immediately want to turn it off. My contribution to *Folkweave* was my first-ever recording, and in my defence I can only plead naiveté. I was doing my best to imitate Luke Kelly, but I ended up sounding like Enoch Powell. It took me a while to jettison that nasal whine, but today I have to try to see it as part of my own musical journey, and stop cringing.

Mícheál came to the *Folkweave* project, having marinated since birth in the rich melodies of Gaoth Dobhair in Donegal. He took the best of Bert Jansch and John Renbourne's open-style tunings and forged his own unique style of guitar-playing. He passed his knowledge and advice to me unstintingly, and though he probably found my ignorance of the traditional scene a bit taxing at the time, he was ever-helpful and a huge influence. His contribution to Irish music is rarely given what I would consider due credit, but for me, he is one of the most gifted and unassuming musicians that I have ever met.

The other albums were called *A Kiss in the Morning Early* and *As I Went Over Blackwater*. Despite my best intentions and efforts, these albums today can be regarded only as curios.

Still, the day before yesterday, I got a call from Guy Clark. Guess what? Guy was looking for some lines from a song called 'Jack Haggerty'. I recorded 'Jack Haggerty' on *As I Went Over Blackwater* and the song was picked up by a band called Touchstone, in America.

'Where in the hell did you hear "Jack Haggerty", Guy?'

'Well, Emmylou Harris gave me this album by a band called Touchstone, and me and Townes Van Zant spend two or three days trying to figure out all of the lyrics of that song. Man, I've been trying to nail that song for ten years.'

I donned my business hat.

'Did they credit me with the music, Guy?'

'Sure, that's why it's you I'm calling.'

Why it took ten years for Guy to call me is for another day's figurin' 'cause I ain't fixin' to start figurin' it out right now.

I don't get calls from the likes of Guy Clark every day, in fact I rarely get calls from anybody. Writers, who operate on the periphery of success, don't even get calls from their agents, not to mind those whom they would like to think of as their peers.

On these albums I was grafting a busy guitar style on to songs taken from books and singing with a voice that carried no authority, since it didn't know where it was coming from. I wrote a polka for the new-born Jessica, and named it after her. It's the only piece of traditional music that I've ever written and I'm glad to say that it has made it into the traditional repertoire. You won't hear it as often as 'The Bucks of Oranmore', but it does pop up now and then at sessions and has been recorded by Kevin Bourke, Cherish the Ladies, etc. When I'm not credited with its composition and it goes down as trad/arr on (put in your own favourite traditional musician)'s latest album, then I'll know that it has truly arrived. Part of its appeal is that it was written by someone who didn't know the rules.

The title track from *Blackwater* is another piece I'll gladly stand over. This is a fragment that my granny sang to me as a child. It has a strange sense of foreboding and mystery to it:

'As I went over Blackwater, Blackwater went over me
I met two little blackbirds perching on a tree
One of them called me a robber and the other one called me a thief
I took out my little blackthorn stick and I hit him across the cheek.'

I sang this morsel to my own guitar accompaniment and drafted in the services of Declan Sinnott to play the electric slide guitar over the melody several times, which he did with great delicacy.

I cite these two albums in an attempt to describe the gradual shift that was taking place, eventually moving me towards writing my own songs. My sources were books and, since I couldn't read music, I chose to write my own tunes. The next logical step was to start writing my own lyrics.

In the Fairgreen, we slept in the upstairs backroom. Úna took an office job in the Blood Transfusion Service, and I looked out the bedroom window. The vista was the Fairgreen field, which was a fixture from my early childhood. The visiting circuses used to set up in the Fairgreen field and I can still hear the high metal ping of the huge iron pegs being driven for the erection of the big top. When Fossetts or Chipperfields Circus came to town, we went to school via the Fairgreen in order to linger and smell the circus exotica and check out the menagerie. I kept looking out this backroom window for inspiration, though I was supposed to be working in the front room. When I adjourned to the front room I became engrossed in the comings and goings of our neighbours. I told myself that I couldn't really start until Úna went to work and my granny went to Mass and the house was empty. I came up with any excuse I could to postpone starting, because, to be honest, I didn't know where to start.

All my pencils are sharpened and my favourite yellow pads are in place, but then the dog next door starts to bark. He's tied up 24 hours a day and the barking starts to grate on my nerves. I decide that it's time to go and have a word in my neighbour's ear, and kill another ten minutes. Over the years, very little has changed. A moment ago I was looking at the keyboard of my computer and telling myself that it badly needs a cleaning.

I realise that I'm not very good at this writing business. I still don't know where to start and I still don't know what to say. But I have a few ground rules.

I'm intent on using my everyday speech, and trying to write about what I know. I don't want to use words like 'ain't' and 'baby' or 'in my soul', I want to use 'bacon and cabbage', 'hurley' and 'Dromkeen'. The difficulty is that the musical soup that I've been supping on is full of songs from the American folk tradition and the modern American singer/songwriters, songs from the Liverpool beat group era, rock and roll, country music, California dreamin' music, and Bob Dylan. Within the brew of influences include my father's repertoire of McCormack, Bjorling, Tauber, et al. My numerous cousins' airings of 'Love's Old Sweet Song' or 'Seven Years With The Wrong Woman', along with my newly-acquired knowledge of the traditional Irish idiom from the Clancy Brothers, Planxty and the Ó Domhnaills. Throw in Charlie Magee and His Gay Guitar of Walton's radio programme fame, along with Slim Whitman and Hank Marvin. Stir frenziedly for 20 years. Add some Randy Newman and Joni Mitchell to taste.

I want to sound like James Taylor and be as Irish as Martin Talty. It's difficult. Trying to put Borrisokane or Hamiltonsbawn, not to mention Hackballscross or Newtownmountkennedy, into the kind of songs that I want to write doesn't work. Why am I not on a train to Manitoba instead of Limerick Junction? Or eating cherry pie instead of rhubarb and custard? Well, I'm not, and the search for a voice of my own will take me round the block more times than I could then imagine.

Úna became pregnant with Jessie. My mother ordered a Moses basket from Delaney, the basket maker, in Gerald Griffin Street. There was still no sign of the tomatoes, though the cannabis plants are touching the ceiling of the glasshouse. *Mo Dhuine* next door frequently and loudly disagrees with his wife; the dog barks. The squad car is called and they try to persuade *Mo Dhuine* to allow his wife and children back into their home. I return from Tom Collins's bar in town to find negotiations still under way and begin to wonder in my semi-pissedness if the Guards have noticed my new career venture in the market gardening sector. Eventually my paranoia gets the better of me and I pull the plants before they've become the real detail.

The writing is a real struggle. I'm like a man trying to break an egg with a mallet. By now I've become aware of the many injustices that I see around me and feel duty-bound to reflect this new political awareness in the songs that I'm writing. Gradually I assemble a bunch of songs that reflect my thoughts on some political issue or another, but they're heavy-going.

'Ferenka': About the mindless effort to impose a German work ethic on an Irish mindset. The project gives false hope to thousands. There's no shortage of *Mo Dhuines* in the management staff. Turns over 50 per cent of the workforce annually. Shuts down in ignominy in 1977.

'The Terrorist or the Dreamer': About the 1916 fighters who were branded the terrorists of the moment, who were deified in 1966, and whose spawn, the Provos, were vilified fifteen years later for dreaming the same dream.

'The Prisoners of the Sheik': About the West's dependence on Arab oil (very naive).

Most of these songs were badly-crafted diatribes. For the listener who sought respite from the daily grind by going to a gig, an evening with Mick Hanly was taxing. I was acutely aware of this. I knew that my gig was devoid of entertainment and since I loved a laugh myself, a sense of flawed conviction, genuine though my political conscience was at the time, pervaded my presentation. The switch in repertoire was radical and I didn't have enough songs to do a complete set of self-penned songs. I found myself doing 'The Terrorist or the Dreamer' and 'A Kiss in the Morning Early' in the same set. The results were incongruous. Add to this the fact that I was going on the odd continental tour with Andy Irvine, for the crust, and wearing only my traditional hat.

Good political songs are very hard to write. Marrying the craft and the message and keeping it entertaining is not easy. Bob Dylan, Randy Newman, Elvis Costello, Dick Gaughan and others all bring it off with style. Woodie Guthrie wrote great songs about mining disasters, lockouts, deportees and the exploitation of the working man. He also wrote songs about 'driving in his car, while the engine it went brrr, brrr, brrr' — light-hearted stuff. I'd love to have been at a Woodie Guthrie gig. I wonder if he threw in 'Little Sacka Sugar' to give his audience some respite. Christy Moore makes the mixing of light and weighty material seem effortless. He can include 'Irish Ways and Irish Laws' and 'Don't Forget Your Shovel' in the same set and stitch them together so seamlessly that the listener leaves the gig with his conscience pricked, and his desire for a bit of craic well satiated. In 1980, '81, '82, the listener left a Mick

Hanly gig with his conscience so pricked that he probably said to himself, 'I could have stayed at home and watched the news.'

During this prolonged period of conscience-driven writing I picked up the colour section of *The Sunday Times* one Sunday morning. On the cover was a picture which took my breath away. It was a picture of a woman aboard a camel. She was wearing a white straw hat, what looked like a brown cloth wraparound, and was enveloped in a gauze of flies. Her eyes sparkled and her skin glowed. The strength of character that oozed from the photograph was overwhelming. For a long time, I couldn't take my eyes off her. She's an Australian and her name is Robyn Davidson. I quote from the introduction to the article: 'In April of last year (1978) Robyn Davidson set off from Alice Springs on a journey for which she has been preparing herself and her survival skills for two years: a 1700 mile trek on foot across the Gibson desert of Western Australia alone but for four camels and a little black dog. This epic of pedestrianism took six months to complete, ending with the five survivors gambolling in the Indian Ocean. From time to time the "Camel Lady" kept a rendezvous with Rick Samoan, some of whose hundreds of photographs illustrate this account from Robyn's diary.'

I read on. By the time I finished the article I decided that this story was worthy of a song. The photographs were stunning. I learned later from Robyn's book about the journey, called 'Tracks', that her rendezvous with Rick involved more than just photography. I'm glad that I hadn't read the book at the time of writing the song. I'd surely have tried to drag this particular twist, kicking and screaming, into the song and taken from the sparseness of the lyric. Recently, I reread the article and noticed that certain sentences are underlined. 'This is me, this is Little Robbie D, and I'm happy.'

This is where I got my hook. I changed it to:

'This is me facing me, all alone 'cause I choose to be,
With the wind and the sun on me, only me.'

I pulled other lines from the diary extracts:
'I dreamed continually of being lost,' she says. 'That string, binding down my panic, began to unwind.'
I converted this to *'A silken thread keeps a hold on you.'*
The funny thing is that I've been telling audiences for years that the silken thread image is Robyn's, and that I actually read this in the article!
The original version of the song has four verses. I had yet to learn that a part of the songwriter's craft is brevity. As you can see from the songs on *Wish Me Well*, I never absorbed that part of the lecture. Nevertheless, before I started performing the song, something must have whispered in my ear that it was two verses too long. Declan Sinnott heard the finished version somewhere along the way and stored it in the prodigious song library that he keeps in his head. It ended up on Mary Black's first record and in other people's repertoires around the country. It became one of my better-known songs.
Some years later, I was in a taxi with Davy Spillane and Van Morrison. Davy and I were both members of Moving Hearts and Van had invited the band to play on an album which he was currently recording called *Sense Of Wonder*. I was trying to impress Van about having written five different choruses for the song called 'Ferenka'. He listened to me respectfully, if a little indifferently, and said, 'I repeat everything.' He didn't elaborate. He didn't need to. I'd heard *Astral Weeks* wafting through the floorboards of the flat above me, morning after

morning, when I lived in Douarnenez. It was strange to me. I asked Regis, who lived above, what record he was playing every morning while he supped his *café-pain-buerre*. With *Sacre Bleu* written all over his face he asked:

'You never hear Van Mawrison?'

'*Bah no.*'

'*Mais c'est un Irlandais. Bah, il est impeccable, ce mec.*'

'*Bah oui, d'accord.*'

I knew the band Them well — 'Gloria', 'Here Comes the Night' — but *Astral Weeks* had escaped. When I did hear it, it made as big an impression on me as any record ever did. It's still a stunning piece of work.

There are moments when people say things that carry extraordinary weight. You're either listening or you're not. I don't think that I heard what Van was saying just because of who he was, or what he'd done, but this piece of information was the reason why I stopped trying to write my life story in one song. It didn't stop me writing long songs, but I realised that there's a lot of ways to write the book, but it all has to go between two covers at the end of the day. Also the importance of having a hook — that repeatable, reassuring line which listeners love so much — started to sink in.

'*I want you to tell me why . . .*
. . . I'm so lonesome every day.'

Now, just in case you didn't get that, let's start that again.

'*I want you to tell me why . . .*
. . . I'm so lonesome every day,
I'm so lonesome every day, I'm so lonesome every day.'

Song over.

Christy Moore also dropped a grenade in my lap one day. Having read the original of 'The Terrorist or the Dreamer', he asked me if I'd asked myself, 'Who's terrorising whom?' That made me think and do some lyrical adjusting.

I was quite excited about the desert song which was to become known as 'The Crusader'. I liked the shape and I liked the music, and it had an unusual subject matter. When I called the song 'The Crusader', I was vague about what a crusader was. I imagined a nobleman setting out on a long journey of redemption with benign intentions and a stout heart. I hadn't heard much about what the brave knight did when he arrived at the dark Saracen's gate, and hadn't cared to investigate. Having read since that the knights in shining armour thought nothing of burning whole towns, men, women and children, because there was evidence of Cathars within, and that the Cathars were reading from the wrong book, my perception of the brave crusader has changed. I don't know Robyn Davidson, but I'm sure that comparing her journey with the doings of the crusaders would not please her. She's been miscast, but I hope that she will forgive my naiveté.

Song titles are important, and if you wait long enough, the audience will give you the title of your song. But I was impatient. Sometimes I'm asked to sing 'The Crusader'. Sometimes I'm asked to sing that song about your woman crossing the desert, or that 'seventeen hundred miles' song. It's taken a long time for the title 'The Crusader' to stick. With due apologies to Robyn, I hope that this recording makes it stick.

Life in the Fairgreen became claustrophobic. The kindnesses of my mother and grandmother became irritating, so we decided to move. One beautiful summer's day, we found a magnificent three-storey, stone house, which was attached to a stableyard in Kildorrery, in Co. Limerick. On the day that we viewed the house, there wasn't a puff of wind, and Kildorrery woods looked majestic outside our back door. I could already taste the fresh eggs and the roasted Sunday chicken, whose neck I'd just wrung and feathers I'd plucked that morning. Úna could see Jessie chasing the wild butter-flies in the meadow and had already started a chapter of her own *Diary of an Edwardian Lady* in her head. A week later we moved in our bits and pieces.

From that moment on I had to chop down most of the majestic wood in an effort to warm the place. Throughout our twelve-month sojourn the wind howled through every crack and ill-fitting door in the house. I also discovered that a working musician needs two cars, not one, to live in the country. I fell out with the local postmistress and couldn't get my telegrams! Telegrams? Yes, telegrams. I had joined the Jimmy Crowley band to keep the wolf from the door, and since we had no telephone, Jimmy had to send me a telegram to inform me of forthcoming gigs and rendezvous points. In a country village, it is not wise to fall out with the post-mistress, or anyone else whose services are essential.

We got poorer and poorer. Úna became more and more dis-enchanted with her curly-haired dreamer who was failing to deliver. I was singing but I wasn't making our supper. The writing was laboured. I had neither discipline nor clarity, and progress was painfully slow. 'All I Remember' got written in spite of all. I did support to Moving Hearts in Liberty Hall in Cork, and Christy latched on to 'All I Remember', and Declan filed 'The Crusader' away.

We moved from the wind-blown valley of Kildorrery to a semi-d in Bishopstown, Cork. Moving Hearts asked me to replace Christy as vocalist with the band, whereupon I upped and left Úna and Jessie to their fates. I thought it was the solution to everything. It wasn't. It was an act of callous indifference, made with the puffed-up selfishness of a mediocre talent. To this day I regret this brutal act of abandonment, but I can't undo the past. Happily, today, my relationship with Úna and Jessie is a loving and healthy one, and I can only thank them for their forgiveness.

Three years later, Declan asked me to put 'The Crusader' on tape. He was producing Mary Black's first album and was looking for songs. It made it onto the record and as I was on the dole at the time, with Jessie in my care, it gave me a much-needed boost.

The Crusader

Verse I

There's a wilderness, a no-man's land
Between Alice Springs and the ocean
Seventeen hundred miles of burning sand
A silken thread keeps a hold on you
When the emptiness like a potion
Tends to fray your reason strand by strand
And there's no more need for the mask you wear
When the last goodbyes have been said
So kiss the cheeks of your dearest friends
Turn to the desert ahead
Now you're on your own like a sailing ship
You're the captain, the crew and the sailors
Turn around and this is what you see

Refrain

This is me, facing me, all alone 'cause I choose to be
With the wind and the sun on me, only me.

Verse 2

You dream so much about being lost
Your ghost by a coolabah sleeping
Haunts you and whispers in your ear
Give up, give up this lonely road
Who knows the promise you're keeping
You can't touch the emptiness out here
But the grace that mends this broken wing
The blue sky to regain
Will lift those feet and raise those eyes

To face the desert again
Let the dawn reveal the journey's end
In truth it's only beginning
And it's as far as your eyes wish to see.

Refrain

Waiting in a crombie (Photo: Colm Henry)

Úna and Jessie (Photo: Fergus Bourke)

When Nobody's Beating
on the Drums

On Mondays the first passenger train from Waterford to Dublin passes the house at 5.35 a.m. If I'm not gigging, I'm up. If I've forgotten that it's Monday, its arrival catches me on the hop, and starts the weekly hourglass again. In winter, I always go to the door of the studio to look at the train. The sight of the necklace of lights snaking its way through the dark is magical. But for the fact that my mind's eye lays down a track for it, it could be in flight.

The train is woven into the fabric of life at Station Road. If it keeps to its schedule, I hardly notice it. If there's a blip in operations, I grow uneasy. It takes about ten or fifteen minutes for me to realise that there's something wrong, then I hear the rumble of the late train, and I've found the source of my unease. If a goods train passes in the middle of the night I feel its weight in my dreams. I'm certain that it wakes me up when it passes, but I never get the feeling that my sleep has been broken. When I say that the train passes within 20 metres of the bedroom, the listener invariably asks, 'How do you sleep?'

'Dad, my bike is punctured.'

   'Oh dear.'

   'Can you fix it now?'

   'I thought that you were skipping?'

   'I was, but I really need to cycle now.'

   'You mean really, really?'

   'Daaaaad. Can you fix it now?'

Katie, my youngest daughter, likes nothing more than a chunk of my time. Not a big chunk, but little chunks every now and then. If she's playing in the garden, she prefers to use the toilet in my studio as opposed to the one in the house. She charges in with a 'Hi Dad', having left it until the last minute to do her widdles. She calls in with broken dolls that need mending, requests for cardboard boxes, reports of dead things in the garden, and sometimes with a story or fact that has just popped into her head.

   'Dad, do you know James in my class.'

   'No.'

   'Well, his dad has your record.'

   'Wow, so he's the one?'

   'No, he has, Dad.'

   'I believe you, Katie.'

   'See ya.'

   'Sure.'

Ellen is only a year and ten months older than Katie, but she is far more discreet.

   'Sorry to disturb you, Dad, but Sammy's paw is bleeding.'

She's now approaching puberty and everything is weird, deadly or cool. They are both wonderful and lovable and so different, they might as well have stepped off different planets. Jessie, my eldest daughter, by my first marriage, who is just as lovable and wonderful, is 22 and has flown the nest. It's only taken me a lifetime to realise that what Ellen and Katie love, more than anything in this world, is Marie's and my time.

Their rooms are packed to bursting with cuddly toys, books, *Lord of the Rings* modelling sets, paints, and a thousand other knick-knacks, that have you choosing your steps with care, lest you damage something, not least your foot, but they gladly abandon all for a family outing. A trip to anything will do, and if I go, then it's really deadly.

This won't last, and I'm not bothered. It has always been thus. One day soon they'll want to cast themselves adrift; when they do, I'm confident that they'll return at a time of their own choosing.

Ellen is already refusing to allow either of us to hold her hand in public. Shortly we'll both be an embarrassment to her.

'There's no need for you to come into the school for me.'

'Can we go the movie with Jenny instead?'

My mother often said that we all think that our geese are swans. GUILTY. Jessica, Ellen and Katie are the most beautiful co-writes that I've ever come up with. They outshine and are more important than anything that I've ever done, or will do. To me, they are more beautiful than any piece of art that has ever been produced, and I don't have to go to a gallery to see them.

Sometimes, when I'm foutering and tinkering with words, I tend to forget this fact, and where my priorities lie. Since I met Marie, my priorities have slowly shifted. Watching her selflessness over the years made me question my own selfishness. She doesn't have to think about putting her children first: they come first. Observing this has brought about a slow turning. I'm no saint, but I think that I've improved, and since the tyranny of alcohol has been removed, I've improved further. I'm getting there.

I'm 54 years of age. I feel as driven today as I did 30 years ago. The difference is that I'm able to put that drive in its proper place. I know what's important to me, and who's important to me, and I try to make sure that they know that too. I don't see the value in making 200 strangers happy on the night if Katie is feeling neglected; or having four songs in the top ten if Marie is unhappy; or picking up an award in the Dorchester if Ellen is wondering when am I going to look at her drawings.

The enthusiastic bunch of amateur soccer-players who flock to the Phoenix Park every Sunday to work off the Saturday cobwebs have a great phrase for the player who dwells too long on the ball and gets robbed. 'Watch your house,' they warn in strong Dublinese. Since meeting Marie, 'Watch your house, Mick,' has become a motto of mine. When I become so preoccupied that I confuse my priorities, I repeat the 'Watch your house' mantra to myself in an effort to refocus. It doesn't always work, but it's always worth a try.

The singular obsession has produced sublime moments of human truth. The pursuit of these moments has also produced countless human casualties. Sportsmen, musicians, painters, businessmen have, betimes, reduced their own flesh and blood to the role of bewildered onlookers at the chase. I'm moved to tears by these moments of truth. In sport, in music, in theatre and in poetry, I'm touched and humbled by the ability of strangers to say something profound to me.

The long periods of physical and mental isolation needed to bring about these moments of truth can be painful to so-called loved ones. It's also very hard for them to express their true feelings in the face of the deification of the father or mother. Many have a tale of woe to relate.

It's impossible for a child to realise that you're in the middle of *War and Peace* and that you're not to be disturbed. Writing, running, painting is something your Daddy does when he's not being Daddy. To Katie I'm 'Get me Wheetos, Dad,' 'Fix my bike, Dad.'

'What do you do when you go away, Dad?'

'I sing songs for people.'

'What people?'

'Anyone who'll listen.'

'Do I know them?'

'I don't think so.'

'Do you know James in my class . . .?'

Katie is the centre of the universe. I'd like her to feel that way for as long as is reasonable.

The work isn't all. Being Daddy isn't all either, but for me it's the more important. The work can be fitted in, and is more joyous, and more rewarding, when Daddy is happy. What makes Daddy happy? The smiles of my loved ones. I feel privileged to have been dealt such a hand. I don't believe that I'm particularly gifted or fated. I have some talent, and I try to work and exploit it to the best of my ability. I'm still searching for improvement, and I now do it when nobody's beating on the drums.

When Nobody's Beating on the Drums

Verse 1
You ask me how I sleep with the train in my ear
Well I don't, I wake up when she comes
Find my dreams again when the coast is clear
And nobody's beating on the drums.

Verse 2
You say how can you think with a child on your knee
Well I don't, I bounce her up and down
I guess it depends on what you want to be
A philosopher, or baby's favourite clown.

Chorus
When nobody's beating on the drums
When nobody's beating on the drums
I find my dreams again when the coast is clear
And nobody's beating on the drums.

Verse 3
I have the ones I love and the ones who love me
They call the shots but really I don't care
I kiss their worried heads, mend their broken wheels
Give 'em all the time that I can spare.

Chorus

Singing from the Book of Job!

On top of the world: Mount Brandon, Graiguenamanagh, Co. Kilkenny

Beautiful interruption

Myrtus Luma

Note: 'Myrtus Luma' did not make it onto *Wish Me Well*. So there is a basement tape after all. Since it is very well received at my gigs, I thought you might like to hear the story of its naissance.

In 1988 I received a phone call from Keith Leadbetter, glassblower, Jerpoint, Thomastown, Co. Kilkenny. Would I be available to do a gig at the Thomastown Festival this coming June and what would my fee be? I said that I would, and my fee would be £300. The date was agreed and I sent 40 large heavy posters of yours truly in a hat, which were left over from my Rusty Old Halo days. (Rusty Old Halo was a country band I formed in 1985. It played for two years, mostly as a residency band in the Harcourt Hotel, Dublin. It recorded one album for Warners called *Still Not Cured*.) Marie Bennett, who was a member of the organising committee, was entrusted with the hanging of the posters that nobody wanted, as they were far too big for the local shop windows or credit union office noticeboard. Frequently, over the coming years,

Marie would remind me of the hardship endured in trying to tie a Mick Hanly poster to an electricity pole near Gowran Racecourse. In fact every time we passed the racecourse:

'I was stung alive trying to get you and your hat up on that pole,' she'd say, as we passed in merry courtship.

'Really,' I'd laugh, as I thought of her looking me in the eye, as the nettles stung her tanned legs.

'Yes, really.'

Today, sixteen years later, this exchange is not wearing the years as well as the Gowran pole, and we don't bother with it anymore as we pass — we've moved on to more recent scenarios.

At this time I was in a relationship with a woman who showed me more love and understanding than any one man deserved. I promptly threw these acts of kindness back in her face with a series of indiscretions that eventually broke her patience. She wised up and took her kindnesses elsewhere. She lived in a three-storey, red-bricked house in Donnybrook, while the basement flat housed her parents. Entry to the house was via a set of steps up to the ground-floor front door. Three nights before the Thomastown gig, I arrived at the steps very badly drunk, a takeaway curry in one hand and the wrong key in the other. When I discovered that the key didn't fit, I became as nasty as a bag of cats. I leaned on the doorbell for several minutes to no avail, so I leaned for several minutes more. With what was left of my reason deserting me, and my curry growing cold, I decided to fly into the house through the ground-floor window. If I didn't make it, there was about a ten-foot fall to the concrete path outside the basement window. There was also a wrought-iron railing on the window, which looked to me as secure as the window of the Laramie County Jail.

I did my Christopher Reeve. My weight pulled the wrought-iron railing clean out of the wall, and the two of us plunged into the basement. Somehow the wrought-iron railing managed to reach the basement path before I did, and broke my fall by encasing itself in the groove below my left knee. Later, it would take 46 stitches to draw the flaps of this newly-filleted tissue together. I was unaware of any damage to my leg, but I had felt a series of bangs as the edge of a two-foot garden wall played an arpeggio on the discs of my back. Through the pea-soup of alcohol, I checked my fingers, which were doing fine, and wondered how cold my curry was going to be by the time I got my act together.

I couldn't move. I could feel the unwelcome dampness of a pool of blood going cold as the curry on my trouser leg. My girlfriend slept on. My daughter Jessie slept on. My girlfriend's parents slept on. Luckily, across the street a gentleman, who was inserting the proper key in his front door, heard the crash, took the trouble to investigate and called an ambulance. I was wheeled into the Adelaide Hospital with a wound that any accident-prone wino would have been proud of. A young student doctor did her best and politely dealt with my inquiries about the likelihood of my playing Thomastown three nights hence. Twelve weeks later, in Tullamore, I barely made it through my first gig since the accident.

Two days after my accident, I took a taxi back to the Adelaide for my 9 a.m. re-dressing appointment. I was still unseen at one o'clock when my girlfriend came searching.

'Let's get outa here or you'll be in time for your next appointment,' she said, whisking me away to her own doctor. With his help I fought infection after infection for the next three months. When I finally got on my feet, I repaid her care and attention by dumping on her. The Thomastown gig was cancelled and my meeting with the beautiful Marie Bennett was postponed for a year. I was later to learn that she fought tooth and nail against booking me for the following year, as she believed that I had taken a more lucrative gig, and that the accident was all a cock-and-bull story. When we did finally meet I lost no time in showing her the evidence.

Twelve months later I drove into Thomastown for the first time, in my old brown Rover, a new girlfriend navigating, and my pair of Bowes speakers in the boot. I set up my gear in The Salmon Pool, checked that the 'rig' was still working, and admired the view of the Nore, which ran the length of the room to the left of the stage. I was looking forward to the gig, but it didn't look all that promising. There seemed to be the remains of a christening or a funeral that was reluctant to leave, and whose kids had turned the room into an imaginary go-cart track. The remains of anything in the room that you're about to play is bad news. Nevertheless, I was looking forward to playing, having a few pints myself, and staying the night in Thomastown, which promised craic.

However, something happened that night which was to change my life forever, and for the better. I met Marie Bennett. It's hard to understand how I, helpless in the wilderness for so long, ricocheting from relationship to relationship, causing grief and pain to myself and to others, suddenly, as though all the stars in the heavens aligned in my favour for a moment, stumbled on the pearl that I'd been restlessly seeking for half a lifetime. Suddenly it was there, within touching distance. All of my senses chorused, Yes, Yes, Yesssssssssssss. It was a new helplessness. It was 'Fall Like a Stone' time and we hadn't spoken one word.

There was a lot of toing and froing over the next few hours, as I tried to angle an introduction. Despite the fact that I already had a girlfriend in tow, I remember boldly taking this stranger's hand in an effort to persuade her to come to Keith Leadbetter's for the post-festival shenanigans. This was the behaviour of a cad, and that's what I was back then, a rake and a cad, and an unhappy one at that. I could use the fact that we're still happy together sixteen years later as an excuse for this kind of carry-on, but I won't, because it doesn't hold water.

Marie didn't come to Leadbetter's, but we had electrified each other so much that what followed was as inevitable as Christmas. The minute I got back to Dublin, I rang Keith to find out who this beautiful woman was and, more importantly, what was her situation. I held my breath. The last thing I wanted to hear was that she was happily married to Joe, and, yes, she was a very nice person, wasn't she? Keith was uncomfortable and protective, so he did the manly thing and addressed me to one of Marie's friends, Fionnuala Salmon. I called Fionnuala and asked her what were my chances, would Marie mind if I got in touch? She said the words I was aching to hear: 'No, I don't think she'd mind.' There was huge scepticism among Marie's circle of friends about the intentions of this Dublin fly-by-night. They were naturally suspicious, and it wouldn't have escaped their notice that I was not alone when I came to do the gig in the first place.

I wrote to her and invited her to Dublin to see a play in the Abbey. To this day she insists that the play was *The Gigli Concert* by Tom Murphy, and though I've checked out the play's runs and proved conclusively that it could not have been *The Gigli Concert*, she refuses to budge. I thought that it was *Big Maggie* myself, but I'd need to have been very drunk to confuse Tom Hickey with Brenda Fricker. If it was *The Gigli Concert*, it would add certain symmetry to the story, as Tom

Murphy, purely by chance, would be my best man at our wedding in Edinburgh ten years later.

Beautiful love letters were exchanged and the courting began in earnest. I couldn't be kept out of Thomastown. It took on a mythical glow — faultless, idyllic — and sure who'd want to live in Dublin, now that it was beginning to choke up with traffic, and I couldn't let Jessie out of my sight, and every time I went to the shop I had to lock my bike, and look at the way the locals in Thomastown could go shopping and leave their bikes outside the pub with the messages on the back and go for a few pints and when they came out the messages and the bike were still untouched: the place was the best kept secret in the country.

The writing was on the wall.

I introduced my daughter, Jessie, who was in my care at the time, to her future family. I caused a seismic upheaval in the lives of Marie's children, Mistley, Ashleigh and Thomas. I was tentative and didn't trust myself. I did one runner and we both spent a weekend aching for each other. Finally I decided to trust myself, and, two van journeys later, had moved everything I owned to Thomastown. It was all sustained by the blindness and conviction of new love. The feeling of genuine commitment that came from both of us allayed the fears of Marie's close friends. It also allayed the scepticism of my own family about the genuineness of my own conversion to a real change of behaviour. Unfortunately, Marie's father Mick kept his distance and we never established any rapport. It was regrettable, but understandable. He died two years later, the ice never having been broken. We grew very tired of looking at the backs of coffins that year. My father died in June, followed by Marie's father in July; six weeks later my mother died. In the space of three months, we were left with each other, Marie's mother having died when she was three years old. It was traumatic, but it brought us closer.

On Saturdays we did the bars of Thomastown, ending up in Murphy's or Carroll's in the wee small hours, getting to where I wanted to be, despite all this love: blasted. On Sundays, we transported the four children and the dogs to an unkempt wilderness called Woodstock, outside the picturesque village of Inistioge, and followed the well-beaten path of the owners, the Tigues. Photographs of the once-beautiful estate hung in Ger's Bar in the village, to which we adjourned after our constitutional, for coke, crisps and more damage for the adults. Woodstock had been a stunning place. The numerous gardens looked beautiful, even in black and white, manicured and topiaried. There was a photograph of one of the gentlemen of the house with his salmon catch for the day laid out on the grass. I stopped counting when I got to 20. Another photograph showed a beautiful, round, glass tea house that overlooked a 40-metre, two-tier maze of path and privet. These pictures were only glimpses of the estate's former glory. There was much more, but it was now overgrown and invisible to present-day visitors.

We held hands like two teenagers while the children raced ahead to check out bamboo land. It was a delicious time. We hung on each other's words, not hearing a thing; just waiting for one or the other to stop talking that we might seal their lips with a kiss. All the clichés applied, all logic deserted.

It's one such Sunday. We've just passed the burned-out shell of Woodstock House on our right and are about to climb to the walled gardens and the dovecote. It's cloudy and a warm, light drizzle is falling. We have colourful macs and wellies and funny hats. I'm still parched after last night's fun despite having had a large pot of strong tea. Today my eye is caught for the first time by the bright orange bark of a small-leafed alien tree. I steer Marie across the grass for a closer look.

I circle the tree and find a piece of three-by-three wood stuck firmly in the ground beside it. It has a cracked, but legible black nameplate. It says:

Myrtus Luma
Origin Chile
1978 height 4.26 metres

I'm no tree connoisseur, but I found the *Myrtus Luma* fascinating. It has small, dark green, privet-like leaves, which are rubbery in texture. From time to time, not from season to season, it produces delicate small white flowers, which look like miniature fairy Christmas lights. Most fascinating of all is the colour and texture of its bark. Sometimes it looks as though it forgot to put on its bark and is standing undressed in its orange skin. Some months later I discover a sucker in the tall grass.

Because of the name-plates, which were planted in front of all the non-native trees, and were now in various states of disrepair or vandalisation, I knew that someone, probably close by, knew this tree, and the others in the estate, and cared about their present welfare and their future. No doubt, they too would have noticed the sucker and maybe been heartened by its sprouting. I could feel their sighs of disappointment at its disappearance. Another act of vandalism. What scoundrel . . . ?

It took me a long time to become a thief. In fact by the time I bagged it and scurried back to the car with it on a rainy Sunday when I knew that there would be nobody about, Marie and I had set up home on the Station Road in Thomastown, acquired an adjoining third of an acre and transformed that particular patch of wilderness into a lawn and shrubbery. It was to the edge of the shrubbery that *Myrtus* was transplanted.

It was an unwilling migrant. It spent the first few years looking sickly and sour. It was brown and spotted and bedraggled like an acned teenager. It was given no help from me apart from a bag of Shamrock compost, a bucket of water and its chances. The miracle is that it survived. Then one day I noticed that, as though blessed by the Aztec gods, it had begun to flower, its acne had cleared up, and it was at least an inch taller. I was overjoyed. I relayed the wonderful news to Marie. She wasn't as responsive as I expected her to be; in fact I got the distinct impression that she was nonchalant at such wonderful news. Did I detect a hint of jealousy?

While the bedraggled *Myrtus* was deciding whether to live or die in the shrubbery, our own relationship was blessed with two new ladies, Ellen and Katie, to swell the ranks of the wonderful women in my life. Around the time Katie arrived, my fellow musician, Philip King, became the father of triplet girls. He concluded that both he and I had sissy mickeys.

Marie and I now had five girls, a bus-load of cuddly toys, a thousand Barbie bits, and Thomas running up and down the lawn trying to dribble a football past himself. 'Past the Point of Rescue' became a huge hit in America for Hal Ketchum and the proceeds helped to provide the space and rations for the hungry troops. The first frenetic rush of love had passed and been replaced by the orange glow of tolerance and respect, deeper by far and hugely liberating.

Woodstock was recently taken over by Coillte and has been wonderfully restored to something approaching its former glory. The specimen *Myrtus Luma* is no longer surrounded by undergrowth and the nameplate has been replaced. You now have to pay to park your car in the turning circle and it costs €2.30 a throw. This is a small price to pay for such a wonderful Sunday stroll. The *Myrtus* in the garden is thriving and growing at its own leisurely pace. I know that I won't be around to witness the orange glow of its maturity. Marie has resigned herself to my conducting an affair with this South American beauty with the stoicism of one who knows true love. I decided that my affair with *Myrtus* deserved a love song. I also bless the day that Keith Leadbetter offered me £300 to play The Salmon Pool.

Myrtus Luma

Verse 1

I have a *Myrtus Luma*, you say 'what's a *Myrtus Luma*?'
It's a tree, a beautiful tree, that's now a child of mine
I stole it pre-Coillte, you say, 'what the hell is Coillte?'
It's the forestry, but between you and me
They're more interested in a lowlier type of Pine
T'was her mother caught my eye
You know how it is when you're just passing by
You see a tree with a bark to die for
Then you see the daughter
I became a baby-snatcher
A *Myrtus Luma* watcher
My wife knows, says 'I suppose
I suppose it takes all kinds.'

Verse 2

I have a *Myrtus Luma*, from the land of Montezuma
Would rhyme so well, but truth to tell
She's not from Mexico
Her parents come from Chile
And she flowers willy-nilly
She might be confused, she might feel much abused
She could be homesick for some Aztec vertigo
But she's far too young for that
And if she threw the towel in now I'd eat my hat
The last thing that I want to gaze on
Is *Myrtus* with her clothes on
One day she will be golden
And a sight to be beholdin'
But as for me, compared to she,
There can't be too long to go.

Angel in Venice: the beautiful Marie Murphy

'A frog came a-courtin''

*Ashleigh, Jessie, Mistley
and Thomas.
Douarnenez harbour,
summer 1990*

Katie, Marie and Ellen

FINAL WORD

FINAL WORD

My finger is nearly back to normal. A small, numb callus has replaced the injury, but the numbness is gradually disappearing. Towards the end of a two-hour gig, it starts to complain, but not badly enough to allow me to stay home from school. It no longer baulks at playing B7, so I'm back to strumming happily for a couple of hours a day, and the grass is two feet tall.

Once more I've been dealt a lucky hand, and I realise how blessed I am to be able to pick up where I left off before the blades did their worst. The album is in the can and the mixing starts tomorrow. I won't be there, as I'm unable to sit through this process with 'mixers' ears'. I can't stop myself constantly dissecting the sound and performance of my own vocal, and am therefore of no help. I'm also unable to hear the clicks and glitches that those blessed with 'mixers' ears' can hear.

Recently, Declan stopped the rough mixing of a track, because he heard an alien sound. No matter how hard I listened, I was unable to hear it. When it was finally isolated, it was found to be the sound of a lyric sheet moving on a music stand, having been gently lifted by a puff of wind, and fallen back into place. When he pinpointed this for me, not alone was I not able to recognise it for what it was, but I was still unable to hear it, so I went and made the coffee.

When the mix is done, I'll probably listen to it until every nuance is etched on my brain, then I'll never put it in the machine again. Hopefully, I'll hear tracks from it now and then on the radio, and be happy with what I'm hearing, but that's not guaranteed.

To you the listener, reader, would-be songwriter, would-be writer, I hope that you enjoy the record and these sleeve-notes. If you've handed over your cash, I hope that you feel that you got value for money. If you've managed to slip a copy inside your coat and leave the store unmolested, please bring the money to the stage door of my next gig. If you're looking for clues as to how to write songs, or write anything, there are none. But a good starting point might be to sit down with a new yellow legal pad and write the words: 'Once upon a time, when I was a young child growing up...'

Mick Hanly
October 2004

Declan Sinnott: friend, musician, record-producer

Mick Hanly: songwriter, guitarist (Photo: Deirdre Power)